HOW TO MAKE MONEY WITH

ANGEL INVESTORS & ENTREPRENEURS

100

RULES TO GET A START-UP FUNDED

TROY KNAUSS AND MICHAEL CAIN

NAVIS PRESS
EST. 2009

2013

How to Make Money with Angel Investors & Entrepreneurs: 100 Rules to get a Start-Up Funded from the Minds of Investors and Exited-Entrepreneurs
©2013 by Troy Knauss and Michael Cain

Second Edition

ISBN 978-0-9895192-2-9

Cain, Michael G. (1946 –)
Knauss, D. Troy (1971 –)

Get In, Get Out: 100 Rules for Successful Start-up Deals

Summary
ISBN (see above)
1. Investing
2. Entrepreneurship
3. Business

Printed in the United States of America
10 9 8 7 6 5 4 3 2 1

Dedication

To our families for all the sacrifices made with every company, new investment and start-up we were involved with. Being raised in a family of entrepreneurs and investors is the best education one can get. Special thanks to our grandparents and parents for giving us the freedom to be successful.

Acknowledgement

Thanks to Judith Freeman, Kimberly Knauss, Tyler Knauss, Drew Knauss, and Phillip Planes for their thoughtful review of the book. This book would be impossible without the work and invaluable insights of Jon Obermeyer, as Editor, and the creative-mind of John Miller, as Book Designer. Special thanks to Barbara Cain, Bill and Barbara Knauss, and Donald Knauss for being so supportive over the years. Additional thanks to all of our portfolio companies and co-investors for learning with us along the way and for staying focused on your exits!

Contents

RULES TO STRUCTURE A GOOD DEAL FOR EVERYONE

RULES WHEN RUNNING THE COMPANY & LOOKING FOR AN EXIT

Foreword

This book is for any accredited private investor who believes he can contribute his money, time and experience to create meaningful returns.

This book is for you even if you don't understand biotechnology or high-tech investing. There are many other lucrative industries worth investing in, including energy, business services and manufacturing deals.

This book is for anyone who lives and works in middle America, one who may think that angel investing is easier on the West or East coast. It isn't easier. It's just different.

This book is for those of you who don't want to go it alone, who want to co-invest with other angels in order to share risk, due diligence and expertise.

This book is for people who have already run successful companies and want to stay challenged, and perhaps find a new opportunity among the tens of thousands of angel investments that occur each year in the United States.

This book is also for entrepreneurs who want to understand and align with how angel investors think, especially the sophisticated ones who co-invest with other angels and other angel funds.

This book is also for students who may look at the marketplace and believe that their talents, passion and drive are better served by starting, growing and selling companies; students who one day will become angel investors based on the wealth generated from their entrepreneurial efforts.

Start-ups are challenging investments and are therefore better addressed as a team sport. There is not only safety in numbers; there is greater opportunity and more enjoyment.

We have done it ourselves as individual angels and as angel fund managers over the past 20 years. We have done it as entrepreneurs and have multiple successful exits among the three of us. Recently, we went out and started (and sold) a successful company just to prove to ourselves that it can be done from both sides of the table in today's economic environment.

While we encourage you to **get in** and **get out** of each deal at the optimal time of exit, we also hope you will settle in comfortably to early-stage angel investing and find it fulfilling for many, many years ahead. Remember, whether you are an entrepreneur or an investor, some rules or guidelines are meant to be broken.

D. Troy Knauss
troy@troyknauss.com

Michael G. Cain
mgcain@angelresource.org

www.100rules.com

MICHAEL CAIN and TROY KNAUSS are available for select seminars and lectures. To inquire about a possible appearance, please contact the authors of *How to Make Money with Angel Investors* at tknauss@angelresource.org.

Introduction

This book is designed to provide an overview of early-stage angel investing from both the investors' and the entrepreneurs' perspectives. The goal is to help entrepreneurs learn what it takes to find the right Angel Investor willing to write a check and to help the Angel Investor find the right entrepreneur to back. While both parties are coming at the deal for different purposes, each shares the common goal of making money. In our humble opinion, it is critically important for both parties to understand the needs, triggers, and expectations of the other in order to be successful. The 100 rules we discuss in the book are not, by any means, the only rules or guidelines for early-stage investing. There are thousands of rules that are constantly changing around the world and even from one region of the country to another. The truth is, with a little experience and luck, you will know very quickly if investing or raising money in this class of investment is something you enjoy doing and something where you can make money.

FROM THE INVESTORS PERSPECTIVE

Imagine sitting down in your favorite chair and looking out the window admiring your perfectly manicured lawn and realizing that you don't have a care in the world. Why not? You've been successful and you should be proud of it. You've managed your money well and can pretty much do what you want, when you want. But then again, something appears to be missing. You don't feel as productive as you once were. You want to do something exciting again. You want to feel needed. Well, there is a whole world out there made up of wannabe entrepreneurs with dreams and visions, but no way of funding it. That's where you may be the perfect fit. You have money, you have great business acumen, and all you are missing is finding the perfect ride with a team of start-up junkies ready to build a company. If you find it, why not take your money and start investing as an angel? Yes, it can be hard. Yes, it can be risky. But, it can also make you and the entrepreneur you are backing a lot of money.

As you can imagine, finding your first deal and stepping up to the plate for the first time can be both exhilarating and daunting. Hopefully, you took the advice of your friends and joined a professionally-managed angel group, or, at the very least, decided to co-invest with other accredited investors in order to share due diligence and mitigate some of the risk. As a first-timer, it's easy to become enamored by the entrepreneur sitting across the table from you with big plans and an unbelievable technology. The most experienced investors will tell you stories about amazing products that defied the laws of physics. But use caution, reality is much different than a concept. It's tough to take something on paper and turn it into a viable product in a market where real customers are willing to pay real money.

FROM THE ENTREPRENEURS PERSPECTIVE

There are thousands of entrepreneurs with great ideas and an ability to see markets before they develop. Unfortunately, there are only a few entrepreneurs who have the ability to get the funding in place to make those ideas a reality. That's why it is critically important to understand, as an entrepreneur, what investors are looking for. While many books will tell you to focus on showing an investor how your company can get from zero to $50 million in sales, the best and brightest early-stage investors know that such a trajectory isn't probable. As you will discover from reading this book, building a great company to create a great return takes a team effort. Make sure your investors want to be a part of your team and let them help you from day one. Remember, there are many more entrepreneurs than investors, so be prepared to have to work at finding one who is willing and able to support your vision.

RULES FOR INVESTORS THAT IMPACT DEALS & WHAT ENTREPRENEURS SHOULD KNOW

ENTREPRENEUR PERSPECTIVE

1

Diversify your portfolio

Don't put all your eggs in one basket. Don't be a "one and done" investor. When you invest in publicly-traded stocks, do you limit your investment to only one company, or even to one sector? The answer is most likely no. As you have learned over time, and possibly from bad experiences, you need to diversify your investments to spread risk and avoid a complete collapse in the value of your portfolio. As an early-stage or start-up investor, you need to apply the same lessons to your angel deals.

It's very easy, as a new or inexperienced angel investor, to limit the type of deals you participate in to a particular industry or a defined geography. You may only want to invest in biotechnology, software, or maybe medical devices because it is comfortable to invest in what you know. As a successful businessperson, you may want to stay close to home and give back to the community where you made your money. What is important to know is that diversification, through different types of companies and different regions, will provide you the greatest chance of realizing solid returns over time.

Let's consider geographical diversification. If you live in a part of the country outside of California, Massachusetts (Boston), New York City, or Texas (Austin), the number and quality of deals that you see may be lower. It's a fact that the best entrepreneurs with the best start-up companies tend to go where the money is. This is not to say that great deals aren't available elsewhere. It just means there are fewer of them to find, and more hay to sort through before finding the needle.

If you plan on being active and participating on every board of each portfolio company, then you will need to keep your geographic approach to a 3 or 4 hour drive in order to maintain some level of active monitoring. Remember, while you are mitigating the monitoring risk, your portfolio diversification risk increases. What happens if there is a regional slowdown as a result of economic shift or "Act of God?" As an investor, you really should consider making some investments outside your geographical preference even if it means not being as active on the board. Use your ability to syndicate and co-invest with angels in other parts of the country who are like-minded and understand the need to actively monitor their portfolio companies.

Now, let's consider industry focus risk. Truthfully, investing in an industry that you understand, and one that you have a network of business associates to help with due diligence and an exit, is a significant advantage. However, it's important to recognize that the deals you see are only a fraction of what's going on around the world. Thousands upon thousands of entrepreneurs, even in third-world countries, are working on the same issues that we are. If your state recently decided to invest $100 million in a state-of-the-art nanotechnology center, does that automatically mean it will have the best entrepreneurs? The best ideas? The highest ability to build a sustainable and growth company? The answer is no, no, and no! Economic developers around the country, and around the world, think they have the secret sauce. For every new center built, there is already one built in five other states and ten other countries. Don't fall into the trap of investing in deals that look good in your region. You need to explore other areas and industries to make sure you aren't getting the wool pulled over your eyes.

Spread your investments around and keep your portfolio reasonably balanced. Associating with other angels and syndicating with other angel groups can help solve your diversification challenges. Expand your network to see a few more deals in different industries. Don't lock-in to a single niche.

For the Entrepreneur

You may have done everything right. You put together a credible investment opportunity, with all the elements in place. You pass through screening and due diligence easily. Yet, ultimately, you are not funded by your local angel.

It may not be about you. You may represent a good overall deal but not the right deal for the angel's diversification strategy. It could be industry-based. Perhaps the angel already has seven medical device deals in a portfolio of ten companies; adding your medical technology would only create a higher level of concentration risk.

It could even be geographically-based reasoning. Perhaps the angel wants to balance an existing number of local deals with a few deals in another part of the country. It could also be about timing and the staggering of potential exits. Take the initiative and ask early on where the angel thinks your company fits in their portfolio strategy.

> **Takeaway:**
> **Portfolio Diversification**
> When dealing with high risk investments, you should diversify your portfolio of early-stage companies whenever possible. You can diversify by geography, industry, potential exit timeline and the size of deals. It's easier to diversify when you make investments in multiple companies; be prepared to invest in more than ten deals to make sure you have enough shots on goal for the best returns.

2

No two deals are the same

Most angels look at ten to twenty deals a year, while more networked angels will see hundreds of deals. But no two deals are ever alike and there's no guarantee that seeing more deals actually helps with returns. Consider the following different variables in each deal:

Investors: You may invest on your own, conducting all the due diligence and taking all the risk. On other deals, you might network and invest with other angels in order to share due diligence and mitigate risk. You might syndicate a deal with another angel group or fund that has experience in that industry. Having the same investors in a deal is rare. Losing just one investor in your next deal will change the dynamics.

Management: Most frequently, you'll back a founder and management team with limited experience. You trust them, believe they are coachable and everyone understands that an exit is the definition of success. Other times you'll invest in a team that needs close board monitoring and ultimately has to be replaced before an exit.

Market: There are many different types of markets and niches. An entrepreneur may have found a new way to extract economic value quickly from a mature market that others have overlooked or from a new opportunity that relies on innovative and disruptive technologies.

Changing consumer preferences and behaviors: Consider that between the time you invest and the time the company starts selling a product or service, the entire market can and most likely will change. Can the management team adapt to these outside influences?

Ultimately, it is important to always focus on each deal independently and not try to justify your investment decision on a successful deal from the past. As you build your portfolio, don't assume anything; make sure you conduct full due diligence on every deal before you write the check.

For the Entrepreneur

Step back and take the time to thoroughly view your company from the investor's perspective. Angels typically fund less than 10% of the deals they see, so make sure you stand out right away as someone who instills confidence. A basic level of sincerity can make your deal more distinctive than the product, technology or market opportunity your company represents.

Anticipate every possible aspect of the investor's scrutiny that may be different than the scrutiny that was received from other investors. You want your deal to stand out more than the three or four other deals that your potential investors are vetting. What management and reporting systems have you already put in place to increase an investor's comfort level and to mitigate risk? Have you set a fair valuation for the company? Will there be any surprises during due diligence? Are you coachable? Will it be easy for you and your team to work with a hands-on board all the way through to an exit? Will the investor feel strongly enough about the deal to syndicate it with other angels? Always be prepared to address investor concerns about how your deal is different from the ones that burned them in the past. Be proactive, don't be afraid to ask them what went wrong in other deals.

Takeaway
Enjoy the variety and opportunity that each new deal represents. Every deal is different and every deal needs to be vetted before writing a check.

Treat friends like friends, and money like money

As an early-stage investor, you should always remember that there is a better than even chance that you are going to lose some or all of your money on any given investment. Would you want to lose a friend over a deal too? So, how do you navigate a deal where the entrepreneur may have raised money from "friends and family"? That early money possibly helped the company organize, file a patent or build a prototype and provided some form of compensation for the founder along the way. However, those friends and family members may now adversely affect subsequent rounds of financing the company. There could be several challenges in place that have already set up the deal for failure.

Entrepreneurs who accept friends or family investments may be setting up the company for fundraising challenges later on. Did the founder give "better" terms to friends and family? In reality, they may have set their investment at an artificially high pre-money valuation. The friends and family won't see an entrepreneur sitting across the table, they'll see a friend. They won't be as diligent as an early-stage angel or angel group would be. The seed investors took the deal at face value because they didn't understand the risk, they were helping out a friend. This could cause major problems for the entrepreneur and his friends once a formal angel group or venture capital round of funding is initiated. Do you want to be involved in this deal?

From a family and friend investor standpoint, chances are good that everyone in that seed round of funding is going to get crammed down when a formal angel or institutional investment round occurs. The next round investors do not want to overpay just because the entrepreneur set the wrong pre-money valuation in the seed stage. The previous investments may have created too many complications for the next round of investors to be able to invest. As an investor, you need to complete early due diligence by asking for prior deal documents and a capitalization table to quickly determine whether there could be potential structural or legal issues.

For the Entrepreneur

At the earliest stage, an entrepreneur often asks friends or family to invest in his company. Today, there are a lot of different ways to go about raising funds, including grants and crowd-funding. If somebody is offering you money now, you usually take it because he may not offer it later. Fueling the idea and spreading the risk is critical, but you should also understand the implications when non-accredited investors, like friends and family, invest in a start-up. They can lose most of their equity when a formal angel round happens, or they can keep future rounds from happening altogether.

Understand, before you go out for angel funding, how accredited investing works. Find a mentor or angel who can informally show you how to utilize a capitalization table, who can walk you through each round of funding to see how valuation, ownership and vesting percentages change. You owe that to your company and to your very first investors.

Takeaway
Investments from the entrepreneur's friends and family members could adversely affect the next round of financing. Watch for complications from earlier rounds that could impact your investment.

Definition of Cram Down
A financing round at a valuation less than a previous round of investment. The ownership of previous investors will be diluted significantly.

Only risk money you can afford to lose

It's tough to be a private investor in start-ups if your mindset is that all early-stage investments will fail. Thankfully, the good news is not all investments are going to end poorly; the bad news is that most of them will. There are plenty of investors who, with a little luck and the ability to follow strict investment guidelines they set for themselves and the best practices now starting to pervade the early-stage angel community, will have a number of positive exits that more than offset the losers. It's okay to start with the expectation of failure and eventually find a way into a deal where you can see yourself, your co-investors, and the entrepreneur making a lot of money. You can easily walk away from any idea, especially if you don't see the roadmap to a positive exit.

The trick is learning how to mitigate the inherit risks involved with each deal and then applying that learning to your decision-making process on future deals. Reduce the size of your bet by diversifying your portfolio with at least ten early-stage investments. Learn to take emotions out of each deal. Don't become attached to a company or an entrepreneur. Get in and get out as quickly as you can. Make sure you and the entrepreneur both agree on the vision about how his time and your money will make a return for both of you.

Deals fail for a number of reasons: the company runs out of cash, you or other investors lose faith in management, the founder leaves for another start-up, the bank calls the loan, the government changes regulations in the industry, a competitor creates a better product, and so on.

The longer a company stays in your portfolio, the lower the chance you'll have an exit, let alone an exit with a positive return. Holding on until the company revenues reach $100 million, or until you get a 100x return on your investment, adds to the risk. You don't want to have so much of your capital tied up in your portfolio companies to a point where you can't invest in new deals that you really like, or in deals that allow you to syndicate with other investors to help mitigate future risk.

To succeed in the face of such great odds can and will be very rewarding. Learn from the measures that you take to mitigate risk for one company and apply that to every company in your portfolio. Yes, you will strikeout with some deals, but you only need one home run (or a series of doubles – even a few "hit by a pitch!") to be a successful start-up investor.

For the Entrepreneur

Angels are willing to risk their money, invest time and energy, and open up their networks to receptive start-ups. This means you have a great responsibility during the time period between the funding round and the exit event.

If you expect a hands-off approach and limited involvement from your backers, then you should seek other sources of funds, if you can find them. If you are looking to create a permanent job for yourself and the members of your management team, then an angel's risk-profile is not for you. You are better off starting a lifestyle business or getting a job with a large company.

If, however, you believe that what you have started could attract the attention of a strategic acquirer in three to five years, and you are open to the guidance of experienced business people (along with a sliver of their personal wealth), then keep reading this book to understand what investors are looking for.

Takeaway
Given the high odds for early-stage deal failures, make sure you thoroughly vet every entrepreneur to ensure that he or she is fully aligned with you to drive the business toward an exit. If not, don't do the deal, even if you can afford to lose money.

5

Don't say "control" when talking with entrepreneurs

If your founder is coachable, consistently communicates and has exit goals aligned with yours, you'll rarely have to resort to command-and-control mode. If the quarterly financial statements are delivered on time and with minimal variances to the plan, then your board can spend less time on monitoring and more on building value. You're definitely not getting involved as an investor in start-ups because you miss supervising people. Let somebody else be the "heavy" or the "hall monitor." You're interested in the opportunity to diversify your personal wealth, learn new industries and work with interesting peers who have much in common with you. Maybe you've already had business success and you want to help others achieve it. Maybe you want to find and be the first investor in the next Facebook, Starbucks, Google, or Apple. Prospecting for an amazing company is challenging and a lot of fun.

While you're ready to be hands-on with the entrepreneur, you'd rather be looking forward, assembling the right board members for each phase of the business, identifying potential acquirers and designing the optimal exit. You're not interested in controlling the day-to-day activities.

This non-invasive approach is ideal for working with many early-stage founders and the management teams they want to attract. For the first time in their careers, they are enjoying the independence to determine their own destiny and to prove their worth in a risky, yet creative environment. Some founding teams will revolt under a heavy-handed approach. Make sure fellow investors and the board members you collectively appointed understand this. You will find that when there is constant calibration involved, driven by both formal board monitoring and informal communication, it won't be necessary to step on an entrepreneur's toes. Be a mentor to the entrepreneur and let him know you are here to help. If an entrepreneur doesn't respect that, it's okay to remind him whose money is supporting his endeavor.

For the Entrepreneur

You've agreed to funding and to a philosophy. By the time you are backed by a sophisticated angel or an organized angel group, you have aligned interests and accepted the key trade-offs:

1) If you get your investors to a near-term exit without the cram-down and dilution associated with venture capital funding, you get to start another company.

2) If you are coachable and accept your board's expertise, guidance and advice, then your dream has the boost it needs to get to market.

You're a self-starter with a lot of energy and motivation; you're not looking for someone else to control your idea. Yet that's what you'll get if you run through the angel money and a venture capitalist steps in. You'll have a lot more restrictions in place, your equity will drop, and you could wind up out of a job. Alignment with angels means you keep your role as leader.

Takeaway

Entrepreneurs can control their own deal, especially if they have a history of success. Until then, most entrepreneurs need to be willing to let investors be actively involved in the deal to ensure a successful exit.

6

Learn to mitigate investment risk

The job of a great lawyer is to lower risk for their clients. The best lawyers tend to be gray-haired and experienced in drafting multiple contracts, negotiating term sheets, and writing related deal documents. The job of a great surgeon is to lower the risk of post-surgery complications. Would you rather have a surgeon just out of medical school or one who has performed similar surgeries for twenty years? As an investor in start-up deals, experience, following best practices and learning to collaborate with other like-minded angels will help you lower the risk that is inherent in this investment class. As an accredited investor, you understand that there is no guarantee of a return when putting money into a private company. If you back an entrepreneur who grasps this concept, it will be possible to leverage risk toward a highly positive return. The rewards should be worth the risk; if not, stay away from the deal.

As part of the learning curve, investors need to recognize that risk mitigation is a mindset and a specialized business skill you can learn and master with practice. Here are five examples:

*To compensate for a start-up company's limited operating history, you co-invest with experienced business people to assist you with due diligence, term sheets, board monitoring, and exit negotiations. Working with partners helps lower the overall risk of the deal.
* To offset a start-up's limited resources, you give the entrepreneur access to your network. Maybe someone you are connected with has access to a marketing firm willing to perform a service for equity versus cash. Finding deals like this helps lower funding risks.
* To diminish the risk of a management issue, there is a contingency plan in place for you or a board member to step in and run the company if anything happens to the entrepreneur. Whether it is health-related, the founder's work ethics, or a bus hit him crossing the sidewalk, investors need to plan for all scenarios. On that note, don't forget about adding key-man life insurance and disability insurance policies on the management team in the term sheet; you will need that money to find a permanent replacement.

* To further reduce risk, you conduct independent research studies on buying habits of potential consumers during the due diligence stage. Ask family members or friends what they think about the product. You may even call in a favor or two and ask potential distributors or retail store buyers to provide feedback. Knowing what actual buyers think before you invest will lower the risk in the deal.
* To lessen market risk, you identify and secure an independent board member who has deep experience in that particular industry and is willing to use his or her connections to help promote the concept.

Mitigation is all about having the insight to find potential issues that could easily derail a company at any time during its lifecycle and learning to offset those issues with the right people and processes. If an issue will prove to be too difficult to solve, it's better to discover that now before an investment is made. Unfortunately, you can never completely eliminate risk; you can only mitigate it.

For the Entrepreneur

Here's how it looks from the angel's perspective. The name on your business card says "Unknown Quantity." Your address reads "Tank City." Your elevator pitch reeks of risk. Every slide in your pitch deck triggers a fear of potential exposure and value erosion. Your prototype works, but can you scale production in a global manufacturing environment? You've sold twenty-five units so far; can you sell two-hundred and fifty thousand? Will a sales team have the incentive to sell it? Your marketing campaign is in place, but is there a large enough market?

Amazingly, this can all be addressed and mitigated. It takes a specialized form of capital, deployed by angel investors. It involves the understanding that the company will be sold to a strategic acquirer, not held onto indefinitely until it becomes a "home run" or limps along half-alive as a lifestyle business. Founders should learn risk mitigation along with the investors and constantly be on the lookout for a quick exit.

Takeaway
Experienced investors should encourage entrepreneurs to understand how to mitigate the risks associated with all deals.

Don't invest in every deal you see

It's tough sitting on the sidelines waiting to make the next deal. But investing can be very cyclical. A year or more may go by where the best and most experienced start-up investors won't make an investment in a new portfolio company. It just happens. The entrepreneurial community may not have the breadth of talent, or possibly your co-investors may be retreating due to the economy. It can be highly tempting to jump in and fund the next deal you see, even if it means funding it on your own. Don't do it! Don't invest just to invest.

If you're not seeing good deals, broaden your network. Angel investors, outside of Silicon Valley, Boston, Austin, or New York, who only invest in deals within two or three hours of their home base, are missing ninety-nine (99%) percent of new and innovative deals. Get off your chair and start networking with other early-stage angel investors or groups around the state, region, and country. Attend regional meetings of the Angel Capital Association; you'll meet like-minded investors and gain experience and connections. Attend regional entrepreneur pitches. Get your name out there as someone willing to make an investment.

Once you find a deal, you owe it to the entrepreneur to make the process very tough. Start early. Make the screening phase an obstacle course. That founder should barely feel like he has a chance to make it through to the due diligence phase. You want to see how he reacts to stress and adversity. If he is extremely desperate and has no back-up resources at all, he might just fold up the tent if the screening or due diligence timeframe is too long. Or, he may decide to keep bootstrapping, make cuts on non-essential expenses, sell personal assets and find a way to hang around on your timeline. Yes, you definitely like to see this type of passion and drive, but that doesn't mean you should invest yet. Keep the process moving.

You also don't want to make it too easy for someone who is actively shopping a deal. You don't want to be the desperate one who gets involved in a bidding war, in order to get an auction "win." This is why investing with other angels and syndicates helps you stay disciplined. Seek the counsel of your partners when you believe you are investing for the wrong reasons. Make sure you set tough terms when you negotiate. Don't be afraid to sit on the sidelines for a little bit longer. If you don't see a deal you like, spend more time with your existing portfolio companies. Who knows, you may find that with all of your free time, you may be able to help get an exit or two.

For the Entrepreneur

If you've had a very easy time of it with angel investors, you should not necessarily be flattered by the attention. You should probably be worried. They may be investors experiencing low deal flow and desperate to make an investment, or worse, they may be first-time investors who haven't learned more strenuous due diligence and negotiation tactics.

Conversely, if you walk away from an angel screening feeling drained and exhausted, tested and pushed to the limits, you should take that as a strong sign of interest. If your references are being triple-checked and financial and market representations are receiving extra scrutiny from outside experts the angels brought in just for your deal, the tough love is earned. As a first time entrepreneur, you should expect terms that don't appear very favorable to you. Your pre-money valuation may not be what you want, but you understand the tangible payoff will come upon exit.

Takeaway
Don't invest just to invest.

Every answer should be, "it depends"

If you ask any venture capitalist or angel investor a question, 9 out of 10 times the answer you should get is "it depends." The ultimate goal for an investor is always an exit but there are many pathways to achieve it. Predicting the most successful is impossible. No two deals are alike. No two due diligence efforts will ever be identical.

As you will learn, much of the success of a deal depends on the personalities involved, the founders and investors, as well as the experience of the management team and the independent board member.

Should you invest in a company with a high valuation? Should you invest in what appears to be a mature and over-saturated market? Should you ever invest in more than 50% of a company's equity? It all depends. Every investor cares about something different. Your portfolio diversification can also drive many of these investment decisions along with whether you are investing alone, as part of an angel group, or in a larger syndicate.

What this should teach you is how important flexibility is for the angel investor. You need to be able to think quickly and be willing to change direction on a moment's notice. Your business experience and gut feel will help tremendously. But nothing can replace the learning experiences you get from working with your fellow investors. Just think about everything you need or want to know as an investor. The next time an entrepreneur asks you a question, be prepared to say, "it depends."

For the Entrepreneur
There are certain guidelines to learn but nothing is certain in angel investing. Should you approach an individual angel first, or is it better to pitch to an organized angel group to get a wider range of feedback? Should you seek out a local group of investors or look elsewhere to an area of the country that might better understand your industry or business model? Should you go after a niche or a wider market? It depends.

INVESTOR PERSPECTIVE

With so many variables, you will need patience and flexibility. Your leadership skills will be tested and expanded because of the plethora of uncertainties. There are a few areas where the answer is not "it depends." Should you be completely honest and straightforward about every aspect of the business? Absolutely. Should you drive a luxury vehicle or wear flip-flops to the meeting? No, definitely not.

Takeaway
Add this phrase to your angel vocabulary. Whenever an entrepreneur asks you a question, the answer is always "it depends."

It's okay to distrust venture capitalists

If someone showed up to run the last two miles of a marathon, celebrated victory at the finish line and took home a medal, you might not consider that athlete a successful marathoner. You might consider him a marathon finisher, but that's about it.

As investors, Venture Capitalists (VCs) are not supposed to be in the investing race for the long haul. Their funding partners have a finite period of time that they expect to receive a return on their investment. VCs get in (late), but if the returns aren't great, they'll wait to get out. They want to see a huge multiple on their investment or bust. While individual angels typically invest amounts of $25,000 to $250,000 in syndicates of $1.5 million or less, VCs invest much larger amounts in each company. A VC typically invests $3 to $5 million or more in a single deal. As a result, given that VC funds have gotten so big, they are having a difficult time finding good deals that require their minimum investment sizes.

Angels and VCs are not really alike at all. One of the most notable differences is that angels invest their own money in deals. This could be money they made as owners of companies, as successful corporate executives, or it could be old family money passed down from a previous generation. Venture capitalists do not generally invest their own money; most of the funds they invest with come from limited partners and the source of the funds are typically large institutional sources such as pension funds, university endowments and insurance companies.

Another notable difference is that angels are typically happy to exit in a shorter time period with lower returns. Angels are satisfied with a 3x to 5x return in a 3 to 5 year exit window. On the other hand, some VC funds will need to have a homerun, 20x – 50x, in their portfolio to even have a chance of providing their limited partners with the returns required for this asset class. Anything less is considered a failure.

Because of recent failures, VCs are mostly absent these days in the early-stage funding arena and are hard to find outside of the traditional Boston, Austin, New York, and California markets. Yes, there are some great VCs in other parts of the country, but very few are options for start-up entrepreneurs. In today's world, angel investors need to work together to fund their portfolio companies all the way to an exit. Early-stage investors cannot rely on a VC to help fund any gaps. While it may be hard to believe, angel investors are responsible for funding more companies and more ideas. Just think about a great company; it was probably funded by an angel first. Angels add more than money: they are mentors, and they contribute substantial value from their professional experience and personal networks. As an angel, don't trust your VC friends; regardless of what they say, their funding models don't work for early-stage deals. You can fund a company without their help.

For the Entrepreneur

It works in your favor that angels are more like entrepreneurs than they are like venture capitalists. Some angels have been successful entrepreneurs prior to taking up early-stage investing, and they take an active role in their portfolio companies.

If you are starting a new company, networking with VCs will most likely not help you, nor should you expect them to mentor you in the early stages. It is very likely that an angel fund or a syndicate of angel funds can take you all the way to an exit; allowing you to not even need VC involvement.

If you are funded by a VC, there is the possibility you will be replaced as the top executive along the way. It's nothing personal; it's simply the way VC funding works in order to give their funds the high-returns needed to justify their existence to their limited partners.

Takeaway
Venture Capitalists and early-stage and start-up companies need angel investors. As a group, angels are responsible for the vast majority of funded deals. Just remember to protect your investment from vulture capitalists looking to swoop-in on the deal after it takes off.

10

If an entrepreneur isn't coachable, tell him

When you're at your child's, or grandchild's, soccer game watching the coach rally his team, do you notice the kids that are listening versus the ones staring up in the sky without a care in the world? Well, that's sort of the test you need to do when you meet an entrepreneur. You want to find the entrepreneur who listened to his coach, who was successful as a player, and who was co-captain of his team, a position achieved not because of his athletic skills, but because of his skills as a teammate. You want to find an entrepreneur who is coachable and understands what it takes to set an example and to drive the employees to a win (exit). Sure, you want to be dazzled and impressed by the entrepreneur; his confidence can attract key employees, suppliers and customers, and potential acquirers. But in the angel model, you know that will only take you so far. An entrepreneur must possess a high degree of coachability to be successful.

Here are some very easy clues to determine coachability. If you ask a founder to share his elevator pitch and he drones on for longer than two minutes, it means previous coaching by a mentor has failed! When you schedule him for a ten-minute, eight-slide presentation slot with ten minutes allowed for Q&A, is he off-course the entire time? If he hasn't been coached properly to respect simple instructions, how can he possibly benefit from your advice after you've invested $100,000?

Does he look you in the eyes when he speaks to you? Is his body language open and engaging? When you or other angels speak to him, does he consistently interrupt you before you finish? Has he already formulated an answer without even considering what you've said? After he hears your advice, does he relate it back to you to let you know that he understood exactly what you were saying to him?

Make coachability part of your due diligence. Ask the entrepreneur's references if they are coachable, and if the answer is "yes," make the reference give you specific examples. When someone is coachable, the coach remembers because it's usually such a rare event. A coachable entrepreneur will thank you for the advice and will most likely coach others in the organization to meet the expectations of the investors. Yes, you want to have a hard-charging dynamo at the helm, but you also want an entrepreneur who exhibits humility, gratitude, and respect. That's what you're really backing in order to get to an exit.

For the Entrepreneur

Most books devoted to entrepreneurship insist that founders exhibit high levels of personal drive, energy, intelligence, creativity and persistence in order to receive funding. While, in the past, investors may have needed to rely on all of these characteristics in just one person, angels seem to be willing to overlook the shortfalls. If a founder lacks certain skills, boards and angel investors are willing to step in and help.

Every single one of these strong entrepreneurial traits could have a negative effect when you are first meeting with and being funded by angel investors. Simple things like following basic instructions, showing respect for others and not interrupting matter. If you have a weakness, you have to be willing to ask for some coaching. The due diligence and board monitoring strategies used by most angels are designed to transfer the experience and insight of your investors over to you for the goal of reaching a solid exit.

Takeaway
If an entrepreneur doesn't like being coached, the entrepreneur should not be asking angels for money. Angels aren't as dumb as they look. If you're an investor and you don't like coaching, invest your money elsewhere.

11

It's okay to invest in an entrepreneur with a failure or two

Failures happen every day. Failure is a part of the start-up and early-stage deal community. If you are in this business, even for an hour, you will see failures and have horror stories of failures that you can discuss with your friends over drinks. The trick is to learn from those failures and try to use that information for future deals.

As you look at deals, it's okay to listen to pitches from a founder whose previous company failed; you shouldn't see that as a reason not to invest. At least he didn't try to keep things alive indefinitely just to maintain a salary. At this point, he probably knows better than anyone else that getting to an early exit is a good strategy; a lot can go wrong with a business when it is not focused. The founder understands the value of each dollar. Once the funding dries up, the company follows. Don't necessarily overlook the value that founders bring from the wreckage of past start-ups. That experience can be invaluable.

A founder's natural tendency for recklessness or cockiness may have been tempered by taking a huge loss, especially if other people's investments were involved. Hopefully, the failed founder learned the management skills and wisdom that one only gains under times of adversity. You may be able to tap into that mindset, and ensure that your investment is directed to company growth and an exit instead of distractions and unnecessary purchases.

Many start-up companies are launched impulsively and undercapitalized with little thought to having enough cash on hand to see things through difficult stages when revenue lags and the overhead chews up cash at an alarming rate. You should be able to access a level of coachability that wasn't necessarily there before. Perhaps, with the first company, the founder was self-reliant or did not have an angel's network of mentors or functional and industry experts to tap. In most cases, a failed entrepreneur is probably more mature and ready to work with you to build a great company.

You'll certainly have someone who understands risk as well as you do, or perhaps to an even greater degree. You'll want to ensure the founder has retained a strong sense of personal confidence and drive to take on the challenges and opportunities that lie ahead.

For the Entrepreneur

The angel approach allows you to look at your business experience differently. If you've been phenomenally successful, you'd probably be on the other side of the table as an accredited investor. If you've been moderately successful, even with some setbacks, at least you have the drive now to create something better. You're seasoned enough to understand the value of outside funding, board experience and a larger network of resources.

Where it becomes tricky for investors is if you've had a failed business. The company might have failed because of overwhelming economic forces that you could not control. More than likely, you were undercapitalized and you ran out of cash, liquidated or the bank called your note. What angels care about is what you learned from that experience. Did it teach you to become more diligent with financial matters and to communicate better with customers and employees? Are you more coachable and open to guidance this time?

> **Takeaway**
> Don't necessarily overlook the value that founders bring from the wreckage of past start-ups. They can learn from previous mistakes and make their next company stronger.

12

Never invest in a lifestyle business

There are thousands of lifestyle businesses that make millions of dollars per year. But as an angel, investing in a lifestyle business doesn't make sense. Sure, from time-to-time, a coffee shop that charges $5 for a cup of coffee may turn into one of the largest chains in the world and have an IPO making its original investors extremely wealthy. Typically, however, lifestyle businesses do not have the capability of returning a minimum of 10x on your investment. What's extremely difficult for investors is to quickly determine if a deal is a lifestyle business or that high-growth business you've been looking for. You don't want to spend time on a deal that will never provide a return.

Most angels would think that a life science or high-tech venture could never be a lifestyle business. However, if you are in this game long enough as an investor, you will have a portfolio company where the founders are comfortably drawing a salary, relying on grant and contract funding and never truly moving the dial forward. Even if these companies grew rapidly and completely by accident, the founders would never want to sell, and as a result, you would never see your money back.

One of the most valuable services you will provide to entrepreneurs is the ability to show how value and wealth is created when the company is sold. Does the entrepreneur understand what he will get out of the deal when a sale happens? If not, do you really want to invest in the deal? The questions you ask during screening and your intense scrutiny during due diligence will flesh out a founder who is on the bubble between owning a lifestyle business and building and selling a high-growth company. Who knows, you may have saved them years of struggle to become something they aren't, or you have given them the resolve to pursue a larger dream with your assistance. The main question here is, if the founder cannot foresee making any significant money in this business, how will you ever make it valuable to a strategic acquirer? Remember, get in and get out!

For the Entrepreneur

To you, it may appear to be a put-down or even a disparaging remark, to be categorized by an investor as a lifestyle business. If you are more focused on creating a brand and a "going concern" than you are with growth towards acquisition and exit, then a lifestyle business may be a perfect match for your goals. Save yourself and your family a lot of stress and time by not pursuing something that isn't a fit.

If you're truly growth-oriented, pay heed to what investors are telling you with their feedback. Despite your best efforts and presentation, you're still acting like a lifestyle business and it's that transparent. Take time to analyze whether you're packaging effectively what you truly believe. Understand angel "math" and key metrics, the role of board members and how a capitalization table works. Design your company for strategic acquisition. Become successful as a failed lifestyle business.

Definition of Lifestyle Business

A small commercial enterprise operated more for the owner's enjoyment and satisfaction than for the profit it earns or its high-growth, wealth-creation potential. Investors are not so sure about the "quality of life" argument espoused by lifestyle business owners. Investors believe that angel funded deals create an even higher quality of living for the entrepreneur's family!

13

Don't bring friends into deals as co-investors

Beware the pitfalls of "friends and family" rounds from the investor side of the table. Just as you see deals in the screening phase that have been irreparably crippled by well-intentioned investments from friends or relatives of the founder, you want to protect your interests from people you know socially. Given that everyone is looking for an edge in financial markets, you might begin to attract friends who want to participate informally in your deals because of the success stories you boasted about at a cocktail party. Fortunately, or unfortunately, your friends don't know about all of the other deals that tanked in your portfolio.

As experienced investors will tell you, having accredited investor status does not guarantee success in angel investing. Your friends need to understand that this is not the stock market. Angel investing is a much different animal, with unique attributes and approaches. The whole definition of liquidity is different: They will not be able to take long-term "hold" positions or engage in quick flipping tactics. Your friends may have earned their wealth through many means, but they may not bring the experience, contacts or mentoring skills that go hand-in-hand with an angel investment.

Think about it from the founder's perspective. Once the deal has been inked, you want clean lines of governance and communication in order to keep alignment with exit objectives. You don't want investors, because they don't understand the characteristics of a start-up investment, "going rogue" by contacting the founder directly with advice that may differ from the board's strategy, or trying to land a job for themselves or a family member. You want to make sure the noise levels that the entrepreneur has to deal with are kept to a minimum from investors. Entrepreneurs have too much to focus on without having to deal with an inexperienced investor.

So, if you do have friends who want to invest, vet them to see where they can help beyond monetary contribution. Educate them that this is not like sharing stock tips. This is not only more difficult, it's a different kind of investment altogether.

If you clearly communicate the uniqueness and the higher risk, your friends may lose interest quickly or may be ready to be your favorite co-investor; just make sure you keep your friendship separate. An investment isn't worth losing a friendship.

For the Entrepreneur

Probably the most valuable aspect of receiving angel funding is the relationship you will develop with your investors, especially the board members who will monitor your progress, mentor you, and introduce you to other business professionals in their network.

Your management skills will certainly improve, and, if all goes well with an exit, you will be in a position, as a serial entrepreneur, to command larger pre-money valuations and better terms based on your ability to execute. You may even do well enough financially over time to be an investor on your own.

What you don't want are investors who bring their friends along for the ride, especially ones who are meddling and expressing opinions not really in line with the strategy of achieving an exit. Know who's really going to be in your board room and make sure that your investors are aligned and focused on a positive exit.

> **Takeaway**
> Make sure all investors are accredited. If your friends want to invest, make sure they are educated on what private investing is all about. You don't want to lose a friend over a bad deal. Recommend that rookie investors join an angel fund to learn about the various risks and best practices. Invite your friends to group meetings so they can see first-hand what it is all about.

14

If you invest solo, don't invest in industries that you don't understand

Think about the industry (or industries) where you have been successful. What defines that success? More than likely there are strong, long-term business relationships that have been built in good economic times and tested in bad times. You know the landscape, the laws governing that industry and the potential pitfalls. You know about all the industry competitors, the experienced suppliers and the emerging technologies. Your specialization also gives you the ability to recognize a good deal quickly. You benefit from an intellectual efficiency of knowing the shorthand of all the jargon, business models, pricing and margins, and how the field has evolved. You know where not to waste your time and who's not worth talking to.

Now think about other industries: food and beverage production, open pit mining, the funeral home business or orthopedic medical devices. You may know one of these industries well, but your knowledge of the others is probably superficial at best. It's deceiving to think that in this age of incredible knowledge posted online, you might be able to master something with some time spent researching. It won't happen. You won't be effective as an angel if you attempt to be a generalist who knows something about many industries.

Would you trust learning about option trading from a video on YouTube? Chances are good that the information was just plain wrong.

If you're investing alone and the deal matches an industry you know, you can be very helpful to entrepreneurs. You can ask the right questions before and during due diligence. You'll have a better idea of which large companies, in this space, have been making acquisitions, and who is likely to be acquiring in the future. You may even be able to network more quickly to identify an independent board member or an investment banker you'll need who may have even more experience in that industry than you do. It's okay to pass on a deal if you're investing on your own and really don't understand a market. Find something that fits and get in and get out.

For the Entrepreneur

Sharing a common language and frame of reference is important. It will be easier for you to shop your deal and secure funding if you are able to approach larger angel groups or angels that syndicate. It is more likely that at least one angel understands your industry or can access an expert who will.

If you are dealing with a "lone angel" who is not familiar with your industry, there could be several potential problems. Due diligence will be challenging because the solo angel may not know the right questions to ask. Valuation will be especially difficult. Determining the likelihood of an exit and finding potential acquirers will not be efficient.

If a lone angel passes on investing in your company because he doesn't understand the industry, it's probably a good thing he did. Keep looking for a good fit.

Takeaway
Angel networks benefit members because, more than likely, a member, or several members, will have knowledge and expertise in a particular industry. Some angel groups specialize in one or two industries, while others don't limit themselves.

15

Don't sign non-disclosure agreements (NDA)

Never sign an NDA. End of rule. If you are planning to have a portfolio of investments, you will see too many deals in similar industries, and the NDA may force you to miss out on a deal if you sign an agreement that is too restrictive. If you feel that you absolutely must sign one, be sure to consult with your attorney on any documents you sign relating to non-disclosures and non-competes.

The truth is that entrepreneurs who look to protective measures like NDAs are often inexperienced, may be getting bad advice from their overly protective "CYA" attorney, or may just be demonstrating real issues with trust. Reputation is everything in this business. Inform the entrepreneur that you cannot execute the NDA, explain why, and even provide references of current and past entrepreneurs that you funded.

There are occasions where signing a limited NDA is possible if the scope is limited to a specific item in the due diligence. An example might be if a patent hasn't yet been filed and you need to review it in detail to make an investment determination. It may be software code that needs to be vetted for specific features. There are other options. You may want to designate your attorney or an outside expert to be the one to review the confidential material, and then provide a report to you that doesn't disclose the confidential material itself. Remember, the NDA should be limited in scope to the particular item you are reviewing and to the person signing the NDA. The safe bet is to just say no to NDA's and the company, if they require it. You're not an investor looking to steal ideas; you are an investor looking to make money on a deal.

For the Entrepreneur
If you're concerned about having your idea stolen by investors, then you don't fully understand how an early-stage company grows and becomes acquired. The value of most companies is not in the idea itself, but in the execution by the management team, their ability to fundraise, and the guidance provided by the board. Even your customers will add value to the original idea as they test your product or service, refining the features and driving new applications.

     INVESTOR PERSPECTIVE

It's always in the best interest of a professional investor to keep your idea confidential; his money is on the line. Before you ask an investor to sign a NDA, remember the unique roles and responsibilities involved in moving your initial concept forward to a point where another company wants to acquire you. Investors want to build portfolios and get to exits. Your idea is just one part of that program. Insisting that investors sign NDAs will remove you from consideration. You will not be funded.

Takeaway
Don't sign NDAs or any other documents that restrict your ability to investigate and invest in companies with a higher likelihood of exit. If the entrepreneur insists, pass on the deal.

16

Coach entrepreneurs with or without the deal

We mentioned that this should be enjoyable, right? Your contribution goes beyond the financial investment. It also involves social camaraderie, coaching and sharing of your business experience.

You can really like an entrepreneur, but that doesn't mean you are obligated to invest. In fact, your value to the entrepreneur could actually be greater when you are not planning to make an investment. The entrepreneur's friends and families may not know enough, or they may be too timid to offend the entrepreneur. As an angel, you are an objective, third-party with the business experience that counts. Don't be afraid to communicate defects to the entrepreneur about his business plan. Once you have decided that you will not be making an investment, however, do communicate this to the entrepreneur, along with your willingness to continue to work with him to help the company reach a point where others may be able to invest.

Your impact, as an angel, on early-stage entrepreneurs can be substantial. You may have a knack for asking the right questions at a cocktail party or at an airport gate that helps a founder refine an elevator pitch before he stumbles over it during a formal presentation. You may notice something in screening or due diligence that helps a founder realize he would be happier as an inventor at somebody else's company or at the helm of a successful lifestyle business that only needs a bit of revenue and some debt to reach break-even.

You may agonize over not making a deal, but still enjoy coaching the entrepreneur in the process. Perhaps that founder is ahead of his time with the business and is pressing a first-mover advantage that could actually be detrimental if there is not enough capital to support a leadership position. Perhaps the founders were successful in previous start-ups and don't have the foresight to see that they are not going to be as fortunate this time around, through either bad timing or a misread market. You may be the one person who gets them on the right track without offering capital. Being an angel investor is not just about investing capital; you can invest your time and help drive a business or industry forward.

INVESTOR PERSPECTIVE

For the Entrepreneur

Forget, for a moment, the money. Angels can be amazing sources of information, insight and contacts. Many of them are successful entrepreneurs on their own, or have been corporate executives at a level that has made them accredited investors with wealth to invest in early-stage deals. They have strong, functional expertise in finance, operations or distribution and sales that is yours to access for free.

While, as a rule, VCs are typically uninterested in start-ups, angels are passionate about them. The questions you will be asked during early screening could be very helpful as you plan your business. The time that angels will put into due diligence can benefit you tremendously, even if you are ultimately not funded. Maybe you learn that you are, at heart, an inventor, or that running a lifestyle company is the best fit for your career and personal risk tolerance. Listen to what angels have to say about you and your company; they can be great mentors.

> **Takeaway**
> Ask yourself this question: do you enjoy investing in others or do you enjoy running your own company? Some angels, who love to coach, are really just closet entrepreneurs with the skills to have multiple exits on their own.

17

Don't invest in deals with high up-front capital costs

As an individual investor, you should be wary of putting a substantial percentage of your allocated money, for start-up and early-stage deals, into a company that plans on using most of the cash almost immediately. Risking too much in only one portfolio business could adversely impact your ability to diversify your portfolio with enough deals; the risk of failure is too great.

When you have high capital requirements to get a company off the ground, then bank or other debt will most likely come into play. In these scenarios, the company and your equity investment is now subordinated to a third party, such as a bank, over which you have no control. Companies can go under quickly, or require a significant cash infusion when a bank calls a loan for reasons that are justified by the bank but do not always make sense to you. Remember, those with the cash make the rules and, as is the case with any regulated industry, the rules can quickly change.

Start-ups typically need money for things like refining and scaling the production of a product (or service), penetrating the market, building out sales teams and overall company infrastructure to support rapid growth. To put angel money into expensive equipment or creating high levels of inventory is not advisable because the likelihood of hitting your projections will be low, and your cash flow will be constrained.

The company can get into financial trouble quickly if the entrepreneur makes a mistake and misdirects capital up-front to build excessive overhead to meet demand on a business plan that doesn't materialize. Help entrepreneurs understand how to build a business within means. For example, do you really need to hire an expensive Vice President of Sales, when, in the interim, your board members have the skills and the industry contacts needed to identify and contact prospective customers? Do you really need to purchase expensive laboratory testing equipment or enabling technologies, when it would be better to contract those services to a local research and manufacturing firm on a per-use basis?

In the simplest view, angels typically look at whether there is enough capital around the table for several rounds to support marketing, to meet milestones and to hit a value inflection point that could be attractive to an acquirer in the industry. It's tough as an angel to capture enough of an upside on your original investment when the up-front costs are so high. It can happen; just proceed with caution and don't allocate too much of your wealth to these types of deals.

For the Entrepreneur

With angel investing, you're not growing a company in the traditional sense of a business with fixed overhead, inventory and a stand-alone headquarters in the nicest business park. You're taking a product or service with high potential for growth, surrounding it with the right talent, and an experienced board, and giving it small injections of capital to move it along into the market.

If you come from a university or corporate background, you may be used to support departments and state-of-the-art equipment. Your start-up cannot justify those luxuries. Your entire accounting department is now a $12 a month subscription to an online bookkeeping program. You may need to farm out research, manufacturing and sales to contractors on a per-use basis. You will want your investors to have the capacity to put their money into backing your vision and passion, and to provide follow-on rounds that won't dilute their equity stake. Remember, your investors took on a lot of risk to help you get started. It's your job to figure out how to maximize the use of cash to get to an exit.

Takeaway
Investments from early-stage angels are not designed for purchasing expensive equipment and inventory. Make sure the entrepreneur realizes how the investment is meant to be used and ask for the Use of Funds before writing the first check. Monitor the balance sheet to ensure compliance.

18

Manufacturing deals are just as fun, and rewarding, as life science and technology deals

In one breath you are told to stay away from deals that require high capital investments. In this breath, however, you're told that manufacturing deals should be considered to diversify your portfolio. So which one is the correct advice? It really depends on your ability, experience, and focus as an investor. You may have already invested in life sciences or technology companies, or are familiar with these types of deals. You may have invested for ten years or longer, with no wins or exits. As an angel investor, there is never a right answer on the types of deals you should be looking at, but if you've been told to stay in one area only, you need to open up your criteria and to consider your other options, especially in manufacturing.

Twenty years ago, it was easy to see the growing trend of Americans looking for jobs in the service sector and avoiding manufacturing completely. Why work when you can just transfer money around from company to company? Well, as government has grown, along with the inevitable decline in our manufacturing sector, the United States is now faced with the challenge of revamping our once-great manufacturing regions.

As angels, we need to be a part of that transition. It is okay to invest in deals with lower multiples if the risk profile is manageable. It is okay to say to friends at a cocktail party that you acquired or invested in a manufacturing operation. In fact, it is easier to explain what you do in manufacturing versus a life science or technology play where there are words you may not be able to pronounce (and your friends may not understand). We're all for multiple shots on goal with technology deals; however, the valuations have to be correct and you need to make sure you keep your portfolio diversified.

Sexy with huge potential isn't always the best. In a biotech deal, it might be fifteen to twenty years before you see your money; that's how long it takes to get a blockbuster drug to market. With manufacturing, you could exit in less than five years. You may have manufacturing experience and quickly be able to add value to the board, mentor the founder, and even possibly lower production costs by switching vendors. You may be able to support a roll-up strategy within an area of manufacturing, or perhaps the founder has created new sales channels that add value to an existing manufacturing play. The possibilities are endless! Find a manufacturing deal that doesn't require huge up-front capital expenditures and get involved.

For the Entrepreneur

You don't have to be a life sciences or technology company to attract the attention of angel investors. It's okay if the word "nano" is not in the company name. You may have a manufacturing idea where the investment fundamentals are aligned with the angel model. You may have built a new sales channel concept, or perhaps you have access to primary technology and want to manufacture intermediate products for large corporate customers. The angels are out there with this type of expertise, though it may be more difficult to find them.

Don't completely eliminate your concept or company because it is in the manufacturing domain. Your knowledge of a manufacturing and marketing niche could be easily monetized. Find an investor or a mentor with manufacturing experience to help you explore where value can be added and an exit achieved.

Takeaway
Manufacturing deals offer a great opportunity to diversify your early-stage investment portfolio. Use your manufacturing expertise and contacts to build a company that can be flipped for a quick and profitable exit.

19

Make investing a family activity

A growing trend in start-up investing is the involvement of family members in the screening and due diligence process. As a result, angel investing is quickly becoming a family sport! You are naturally going to talk at home with family members about your investment activities and what deals interest you. Of course, you'll be talking in general terms and not sharing any trade secrets.

Sharing your philosophy is a great way to teach your children about business and portfolio diversification, as well as how to measure risk and mitigate it. Your family members, in turn, could contribute valuable insight about the deal; maybe details on the buying habits of a certain demographic that your due diligence team never considered. Or maybe they have used a substitute product that the entrepreneur forgot to disclose. As previously discussed, a great way to vet a product is to explain, in layman terms, to a family member what the company's product is, or you could even have them test the product. It's an educational family activity that gets your spouse, your kids, and your grandkids involved.

As a quick tip, you should not be investing in early-stage deals as a way to buy a job for someone in your family. From a founder's perspective, having the adult children of investors involved in the deal may not be a good thing. Entrepreneurs fear this type of relationship because of the perception of "control." If you hear a co-investor around the table during due diligence say, "I'll put in $200k, but I want my kid to run the company" or "my son-in-law would be perfect for this company," you may want to step away from the deal because the goal of the company went from moving it toward an exit to becoming a family business.

These actions are unacceptable. Any behavior by investors or entrepreneurs that takes attention away from the primary goal of exiting through the sale of the company within a three to five year window is putting your investment at risk. Keep family investing a fun activity, but don't mistake it for an opportunity to create a job; it's not fair to you or the entrepreneur.

For the Entrepreneur

Some investors will want to run your business. Some will want to have their adult children run your business. Be aware that this is a possibility and make sure the due diligence from your side of the table explores this issue. Make sure everyone around the table introduces himself and states his relationship to the others. You'll need full disclosure in order to proceed knowing all the potential risks and "requirements" that come with receiving the investor's money.

Just as angels are encouraged to include family members in the process, you may have the opportunity to tap the insights of your spouse or children. If the company is eventually acquired at a high multiple, there is the possibility that significant wealth will be created in your family for the first time, and you will become an accredited investor. Just think, once you exit, your next question is which side of the funding table you want to sit on. Do you start another company or do you fund another entrepreneur?

Takeaway
Teach future generations to invest in early-stage companies and get them involved early. Family members can provide incredible insights about products and markets.

20

There's never a full drought: drive deal flow with constant networking

While it doesn't happen in Silicon Valley, Boston or Austin, it can easily happen everywhere else. Deal flow will dry up. The regional early-stage investor conferences don't always offer anything new to see. So what happens when you live in an area where you are challenged to find enough deals to consider or the deals aren't broad enough across industries to create diversification in your portfolio? Without expanding your reach geographically and making the hike to an area known for a lot of activity, you must be as resourceful as possible. Look for places entrepreneurs are most likely to surface.

Start with lawyers. Start with your lawyer, then expand your scope. Anyone incorporating a business with the thought of one day raising money might seek the counsel of a corporate attorney or even a family law attorney who then refers them within the firm. You might also find entrepreneurs flocking around intellectual property attorneys, lawyers who specialize in contracts and leases, or even attorneys who practice employment law. Law firms don't typically have independent sales forces, so you can find attorneys networking to build up their own practice volume.

The same goes for accountants, especially those specializing in small, closely-held businesses. Network with accounting firms that sponsor entrepreneurship awards or have a specialty high-growth practice area. If you are a member of a group such as Rotary or Kiwanis, take advantage of your own network and take the time to visit all the clubs in town.

Most areas have at least one business incubator or "accelerator" in place. Some are brick-and-mortar facilities, while others are virtual yet highly visible. Most universities with a technology transfer office or emerging research program will have an incubator located on campus or affiliated with a lab. Sometimes you need to make your own deal flow. If you can capture it before it hits the market, there is the opportunity to get a huge advantage over more passive investors.

For the Entrepreneur

The right investor is out there. There are an estimated five to seven million accredited investors in the U.S. alone, although only about 10% of them are actively investing at any one time. It can be challenging in areas of the country that lack formal investing clubs or angel funds that are easily located in an online directory. You'll have to be resourceful to identify, attract and screen investors.

You might have to meet potential angels through an intermediary, like your attorney, accountant or other business professionals who self-promote in order to drive more professional income. Angels will prowl the halls of business incubators or you might find them at local "tech council" meetings where the topic might be intellectual property or raising capital. There are also angels who are "in residence" and affiliated with a local university, or serving on a university business school board. Angels are out there if you look hard enough.

Takeaway
Visit the Angel Resource Institute (ARI) for a list of active angel groups. Start networking and learning how others source their own deal flow.

21

Angel investing is tough. If you don't enjoy it, don't do it!

As an accredited investor, you have many options. You could choose to play the stock market for a few hours each day and spend the rest of the time on a golf course or out on a sailboat. You could return to running a company. Or, you can dive into angel investing. It will be one of the most challenging things you undertake in your entire life, which probably makes it so appealing at this juncture.

Investing in early-stage companies is demanding and a tough area to see quick success in if you're just starting out with a portfolio. You better enjoy it and derive other forms of satisfaction from it, because you won't know how successful you are going to be for three to five or even ten years. Mentoring a founder or a group of founders across a varied portfolio could be what keeps you motivated. You may find that you become most engaged when you are scrutinizing the deal at the due diligence phase, channeling your long-held belief that you should have really become a private detective or forensic accountant.

Where we hope you might find immense value is in navigating unknown waters. It's taking a strategic leadership role to guide a company through product development, market adoption and the scale-up of manufacturing or services delivery; it's almost like a river pilot guiding a container ship through the shoals and sandbars on the way to the open sea. Perhaps you'll learn you have a knack for getting exits. Maybe you are capable of spotting potential acquirers or industry-specific investment bankers. Maybe you become the go-to person whenever a portfolio company is ready to maximize the value proposition for a quick sale.

What we have mostly observed is the camaraderie that evolves from working shoulder-to-shoulder with other angels. There's a social payoff that arises, especially at the local level. You may live in what you think is a remote area of the country without any angels nearby, and through this process you learn that there are actually dozens. Active angels find that they are able to engage spouses and other family members in their activities, which helps create stronger bonds. Angel investing is highly educational. It can also be highly emotional. It cannot be taught anywhere, but

INVESTOR PERSPECTIVE

must be learned by doing. Start investing and be patient!

For the Entrepreneur

Angel investing has not been around in any formal way until recently. Much of what angels know has been learned one deal at a time, in isolation. When angels came together in a group or in a formal angel fund, best practices began to emerge for a broader spectrum of companies. Standards were created and expectations evolved for due diligence, term sheets, board monitoring and exit timelines with reasonable multiples on each investment.

Angel investing is very challenging and angels derive other kinds of psychological compensation for their efforts. The more you understand how an angel operates, the better your chance of success with your start-up. Learn what the angel wants, be genuine, and you will get funded.

Takeaway
There's a lot to know about start-up deals, but if you learn the core competencies of angel investing and take several companies all the way through to an exit, you'll understand why so many of us can't stop. Always be ready to fund the next one; you never know, it could be the next billion dollar idea.

READY TO CLOSE ON FUNDS? THESE NEXT RULES HELP DETERMINE HOW & WHEN TO DO A DEAL

ENTREPRENEUR PERSPECTIVE

22

Plan your exit before making your first investment

Before you invest in a new start-up or early-stage company, it's important, especially from an investor's standpoint, to vet every deal and to fully understand how you're going to get a return on your money. Investing in start-up deals is not like the stock market; your stock can't be traded on the open market. You are now a shareholder in a private company. To make money, you need the company to have a liquidity event, which typically means you need the company to sell. Period. So, when you are ready to write your first check, make sure you have an answer to this question: How am I going to get paid back?

Exits don't just happen. As an investor, in coordination with the entrepreneur or founder you are backing, you need to have a strategy in place to make an exit happen. Can the entrepreneur take the company from start-up to exit? Are there board members who can help the company expand into new markets rapidly and start showing revenue quickly? Who are the investment bankers out there with the contacts to close a deal? When you align the founding team, your fellow investors and potential acquirers around a common vision of a shorter-term exit with reasonable returns, you are reducing the risk factors that cause other early-stage companies to stall, drift and fail.

If you are new to this privileged class of investment, make sure to find an experienced co-investor willing to share insights and war stories about past deals that were successful or even ones that failed. As you will definitely learn, failures happen every day in this business; the most successful investors understand this before they put their own money at risk. This book, and the rules that follow, will definitely help you determine if you are ready to become a private investor in start-up deals. Good luck and here's to many successful exits!

For the Entrepreneur

You're excited about the possibilities. You've identified a viable market, you understand the pain points and you've developed the perfect solution. You're passionate and motivated. All you're missing is the capital. However, if you're not thinking about a three-to-five year exit, then you're not aligned with the investors who have the best chance of helping you.

Founders who are not exit-focused may spend too much time perfecting a product, when in fact the product, in its current state, will be accepted just fine by the majority of customers and generate the revenue that might attract potential acquirers. Founders who get married to or fall in love with the company they've created will have difficulty disassociating themselves when the time comes to part with it. Your company becomes strongly associated with personal identity and potentially your only source of income. It's better to think exit; you'll have a higher chance of being funded next time.

Takeaway

Every deal needs to identify how and when it will make a return for both the entrepreneur and investor. Hopefully, in your very first deal as an early-stage angel investor, you will do everything you can to mitigate the risk and move the company toward a quick return. Don't get caught up in the product with the entrepreneur; always keep an eye on the finish line.

Founders: Don't start dreaming about how you are going to start spending all those millions of dollars after the company is sold. You still have a business to run.

23

Syndicate, syndicate, syndicate

It is impossible to foresee all future needs of an early-stage portfolio company, which is why it is imperative that you syndicate every investment with other like-minded investors. Syndicating deals opens up geographic investment opportunities for investors and gives the entrepreneur access to additional monetary and human capital. The more you network as an investor with other angels and angel groups, the more you increase the number of potential syndication partners and the ability to share risk.

The value of syndication can be dollars, today or in the future, access to a larger and more diverse network, assistance in due diligence before committing to the deal, or simply just spreading the risk. A syndicate gives investors, and the entrepreneur, the ability to fill out a funding round with fewer trips to raise money and more time focused on the business.

There are, however, some drawbacks to syndication. There is a risk that if one investor drops out before the deal closes, others may follow. The investor base is stronger and, as a result, may dictate more stringent terms for the entrepreneur. Shared due diligence may open up liability for investors, so it may be a best practice to agree to waive liability between syndication parties prior to sharing diligence materials. Investors have different needs. Even though some investors may not like the idea of taking a backseat on a particular deal, the syndicate needs to decide early in the process which investor or group will take the lead. If this is one of your first angel deals, leading a syndicate is difficult; there is a specific skill-set needed that is learned over time and with repetition.

For individual angels, it almost never makes sense to be the sole investor in a deal unless the dollars are relatively small. You need to remember that most investments will fail. Sometimes the failure is due to a lack of funding, and other times the company never had a chance in the first place due to a bad idea or a bad team. By syndicating, you can mitigate some of the funding, due diligence, and monitoring

INVESTOR PERSPECTIVE

risks inherent in every deal. Go out there and start networking with other angels; your returns will be better for it.

For the Entrepreneur

Do you really want to depend on only one investor to help you grow your business? Can one investor be relied on if you need a future round of funding to keep the lights on? The truth is you cannot depend on a single individual investor. While it is almost always in the interest of the entrepreneur to take money when it is available, sometimes it makes sense to push your investor toward a syndicate. As an entrepreneur, you'll welcome more investors because you need as much support as possible. Investors like to help protect (by participating with the entrepreneur as well as making an investment) their money so they are often available to you 24/7. Having more investors increases your network and your ability to be successful.

On the flip side, it is important to keep in mind that having more players around the table during the due diligence phase will increase the risk of investors finding a reason not to invest. They might also dictate tougher terms. Having the proverbial "too many cooks in the kitchen" can be extremely stressful.

Definition of Syndication
The process of bringing together several investors or lenders to fund a company. Investors in a syndicate may be legally-bound to make future capital investments if defined in the closing documents. A syndicate is not limited to equity investors; it can be a combination of debt and equity players.

24

Founders and their deals are not always worth $1 million right out of the box

While we advocate simplifying as much as possible, we find there is consistent over-simplification by founders when it comes to valuation for a start-up.

"How much is your company worth?" Invariably, the answer will be the number of founders times $1 million. Whether the company is at the idea stage, has a prototype or has been hanging around and just needs capital, the $1 million-per-founder formula is perpetuated. Where this formula is taught, we haven't figured out.

Founders think they want to keep the valuation as high as possible, when what is really more important is to align with an investor's expectation of reality and the potential impact on future valuations and rounds. First, a high valuation, from an entrepreneur with little progress to date, shows a lack of sophistication and little thought behind the calculation. Whether it's a life sciences company or a gutter repair business, most entrepreneurs only look at it from their side of the investment. They don't think about what an investor may want. It's strictly psychological. They don't realize that with two rounds of funding and an artificially high valuation, they could be left with nothing. Future and potential investors won't be willing to fund the next round because the deal may be too expensive and they won't want to devalue the current investors with a low-ball offer.

You want founders to understand that they will make their money at the time of exit. So how do you get that point across? You'll want to mentor them and teach them that there are many ways to value what a company is worth at the start. Ultimately, it's what the investor is ready to pay. It's partly a formula, but mostly art and gut feel.

Remember, the initial valuation question put to the founder is a gating mechanism that helps the investor determine if he is willing to look at the project. The investor may not always have it right either. As a rule of thumb, angels have been trained not to invest in deals with a pre-money valuation above $3 million. While that is not written in stone, it is considered best practice. There are some early-stage investors who want to get involved with manufacturing and other capital intense industries that may have pre-money valuations much higher than $5 million. Those deals can be great, but know the risks going in. It doesn't always have to be the high tech deal that returns the most dollars. Don't be afraid to push back on valuation against the entrepreneur; you need to make sure your return is worth the risk.

For the Entrepreneur
When asked by potential investors (formally or informally) what the value of your company is before their investment is made, make sure you have thought through the answer and have a solid rationale behind the number. Demonstrate that you understand the end-game, that the real value of the company is when the investors are cashed-out through an acquisition of the company.

The right way to think about the valuation question goes like this: If you think you're going to exit in five years and you'll need $4 million in two rounds of funding to get there, what valuation today will take you to that goal? Investors spend a lot of time educating founders and talking them down from high valuation numbers that have no basis in reality. You'll be ahead of the game if you can show investors that you understand how to intelligently discuss a range of valuations and show them the returns required on the risk they are taking to fund you. There are some great online tools available to educate entrepreneurs on dilution. Visit 100Rules.com to learn more.

Definition of Pre-Money Valuation
The negotiated value of a company immediately before investors put money into a round of financing. The valuation figure agreed upon by both investors and founders serves as the baseline for the term sheet and determines how much equity investors get in exchange for their money.

25

Money is just as important as an idea

You won't find a stock market to buy and trade ideas. This is not 1998; you cannot take your idea, drawn on the back of a napkin, public, nor have your idea acquired by a Fortune 500 company without putting in some level of effort. It's about building a solid sales and marketing company or proving, with FDA approved clinical trials, a major drug discovery. It's these, not just ideas, that creates liquidity and wealth. Entrepreneurs need to execute a plan to get a third-party interested in a deal. There's the classic: I'd rather invest in an "A" team with a "C" idea, than a "C" team with an "A" idea. It's true, "A" teams will find a way to be successful; they will get to an exit. Many investors and entrepreneurs, in their exuberance, forget this while some are so new to the game they truly don't know what they don't know. There are millions of ideas out there but only a few great entrepreneurs. Even rarer is the ability of an exited-entrepreneur to repeat success.

Just think about an idea you recently heard. How do you know if that idea can succeed? Is the entrepreneur worth funding to find out? What if the product doesn't resonate with the market? What if the product only solves the pain of a few customers? What if the product is too early entering the market and customers aren't quite ready to adopt the innovation? What if things aren't going well and the entrepreneur wants to add expensive and seasoned executives to the payroll instead of using an experienced board to keep funding requirements low? There are hundreds of things you need to consider as an investor. The risk of getting to market is high. The risk of finding the right marketing strategy is high. The risk of having enough funding to compete against other, better funded, start-up companies is high. Remember, ideas are a dime a dozen and they can drain a million dollars or more each if you aren't careful!

As an active, early-stage angel investor, you will be exposed to a lot of interesting ideas, entrepreneurs, and management teams every year. You might invest hundreds of hours screening those that you find attractive. But, no matter how much you screen, and how much due diligence you conduct, the probability of success is fairly low. Your money is what makes a good idea possible. Without your investment, a start-up is just an idea that has nowhere to go. If an entrepreneur doesn't value you and your investment risk, walk away from the deal.

For the Entrepreneur

Nothing happens without money or a money substitute. Even the act of bootstrapping a start-up when you act like you don't have any money is a form of currency; it's still a form of financing.

As you approach potential investors, it's critical to understand what the money means to them versus what it means to you. On one level, it is about creating higher than expected returns against safer and more traditional forms of investment. Their personal wealth could be a way for them to leverage a lifetime of business experience and contacts, and to create even more wealth in a fulfilling way. They may have the interest of teaching their family members about the value of mitigating risk. The money could be the fountain of youth; investing it in early-stage deals keeps them young and their intellect sharp. Be aware of your idea-bias; it's not the only measure of value.

> **Takeaway**
> An idea is an idea. It won't go anywhere without money to move it forward.

26

Trust your gut

It's the bottom of the ninth inning with two outs, the bases are loaded, and you're heading to the plate representing the winning run. You know that anything less than a hit or a walk sends your team home for the season. Being as confident as you are, your gut is telling you that you are going to succeed; you are going to win the game for your teammates. But honestly, you haven't picked up a bat or played in a real baseball game for twenty years. The chance of you actually succeeding is even lower than your chance of making a return on a start-up investment. If you were betting in Vegas, would you trust your gut? Sure you would, because in this scenario you're betting on yourself, not a stranger. That's the problem with angel investing, you are almost always betting on a stranger. You probably never met the entrepreneur before he walked into your office with a great idea and a business plan. So, if we turned this scenario around and had the entrepreneur pitch hit for you in the game, would you still place that bet in Vegas? Your gut would probably say "no way". Welcome to the world of angel investing. For experienced investors, gut feel almost becomes second nature. There may be nothing specific to point to, but with every deal, you have an almost immediate reaction, positive or negative. It's a buyer's intuition.

To counteract this gut feeling, you can try to decipher which entrepreneurs are truly in it for the long haul, and which ones are just not suited for the role. You may, like many professional angels, have specific ways and instructions for entrepreneurs to make presentations, partly so you can compare them to past presenters. There can be little "tells" that something isn't right. Perhaps it's just their body language. Perhaps the entrepreneur isn't knowledgeable about the financials of his own company. Perhaps when one co-founder shows up and the other one doesn't, you get the sense there might be some discord between them or that your group wasn't a priority for the other founder. Perhaps each founder wants to have the salary, vacation and a personal administrative assistant like he had at his former corporate job. Creating and following a process to vet deals will help with investment decisions.

Over time, you'll be able to trust your gut right away. It's not all about the negative feelings. You'll often use your gut feel to say, "Yes, I want to invest." Use caution, however, because some of your best deals may be those from which you thought about walking away.

For the Entrepreneur

Angels can kill a deal at any point in the process for any reason. Given the emphasis angels place on gut feel, your approach with an investor should be as straightforward as possible. Lead with hard examples and hard numbers. Aim for hyper-honesty and avoid exaggeration. Make them want to like you, so that the gut-read is positive and focused on the opportunity.

Here are some common pitfalls: Dressing too casually because you believe that being "hip" raises more money for a tech play (it depends). Stating the valuation of the company simplistically, multiplying $1 million times the number of founders; that equals a low sophistication level and is a no-go. Even something as minor as arriving at a meeting with a large three-ring binder. The investor concludes immediately: if that's your method of organization, I don't want to do business with you.

In order to avoid the pitfalls, make sure to talk to other local entrepreneurs and learn how they managed the funding, operational, board, and exit process. You can never have too much information on your investors.

Takeaway
If your gut says "no," kill the deal!

27

If an entrepreneur lies, pull your offer

There will be occasions when you'll find something materially wrong during due diligence. Most times they are inadvertent; however, if you find the entrepreneur, or a team member, represents some fact you later find to be untrue, you should point it out and walk away from the deal. You and your entrepreneur need to trust each other, period! How do you deal with gradations of dishonesty: the fibs and fudges, the white lies and manipulation of facts? Many times, representations are made about third-party interests in the product or service. These representations often get you excited that the investment is a sure thing. This is where strong due diligence, and checking the facts, helps you sort out the potential for those fibs versus facts. Dishonesty can ruin an investment. If you are lucky enough to catch it before you write the check, walk away from the deal.

It's easy for a charismatic founder to get away with a certain level of fact fudging to get a business off the ground. Maybe he mentioned to one customer that he landed another customer in order to get the business or that he has a purchase order coming; that happens all the time. But what if the founder uses data from a marketing study to verify a niche, but inexplicably can't find a copy of the study for you to review because it was "lost when my laptop was stolen from my car yesterday?" If you get a story that sounds like a high school excuse, go on "Yellow Alert". There is something very wrong. If you find that a story doesn't check out, expect to get a bunch of additional stories that just don't make sense. Remember the old adage, "Trick me once, shame on you; trick me twice, shame on me."

We make a strong case throughout this book for personal interaction between investors and founders. Remember, you supply the money, the connections, and the mentorship. If you can't trust your entrepreneur, it will lead to a failed relationship.

The same no-tolerance rule applies to your co-investors. It's tough to make money with people you don't trust. Once the deal is signed, we advocate spending a good amount of face-to-face time with the entrepreneur, both in formal situations like board meetings, and with informal check-ins by non-board members. If the entrepreneur hasn't been truthful, you'll eventually find out. Hopefully it won't be too late!

For the Entrepreneur

You may think you're stating the facts as best you know; however, think about how you are presenting them. Are your assertions of fact verifiable? Angels talk to other angels. Angel funds frequently communicate with each other around deal flow and due diligence. With the rise of deal sharing sites for angels, the communication levels have risen significantly in recent years and will continue to get even stronger. Parallel due diligence is rising within regions. Deal sharing is rising from state to state. When angel funds syndicate, there are intense levels of group scrutiny. If you become known as not factual, you can ruin your chances of ever raising money in your region.

Take an assessment. Have you been consistently truthful to all parties along the way? Have you fudged the facts to get others to invest or customers to buy? Have you cut corners along the way to accelerate the company's development? If you notice you have this tendency, stop. Dishonesty adds a totally new level of risk and there's enough inherent risk in any deal already; you will not be backed by the best investors if you make a habit of stretching the truth.

Takeaway
Make a point to meet with the entrepreneur multiple times before giving him the check. Each time ask the same questions to make sure the answers are consistent.

28

Never say never when turning down a deal

When you hate a deal, you want nothing more than to beg the entrepreneur to stop talking. You want him out of your office. But remember, you have a reputation to maintain and you never really know if and when one of those entrepreneurs will ever come back with a great deal. You want to build a rapport with founders in order to have access to information that gives you the best snapshot of the company. You might have limited financial statements to review and not much historical revenue to analyze with an early-stage company. You are often put in a position to make investment decisions based on intangibles. You will have invited the founder to give his company its best shot at funding, and strong emotions can come into play if you decide not to fund the deal.

It's important to respect those emotions and the passion of the founder. Be polite and encouraging when passing on a deal. If there is anything that can be fixed, let him know specifically what needs to be addressed and exactly what the time duration should be before resubmitting the deal for consideration.

Here's where you can get into trouble if you blow off a deal too quickly or impersonally. What if you live in an area of the country where deals are scarce? You may have "poisoned the waterhole" for other entrepreneurs with fundable deals. Many entrepreneurs will go elsewhere for funding if you have a reputation for continually turning deals away or not offering constructive feedback. What if your negative reputation with entrepreneurs spreads to co-investors? You will have a difficult time sharing deal flow, screening, and due diligence with experienced investment partners who help mitigate the risks involved with each deal. What happens if the entire local entrepreneurial ecosystem is affected? You need business incubators, law firms and networking events for deals to surface. There are definitely parts of the country where entrepreneurs, and subsequent funding opportunities, are lagging. Don't let the behaviors of investors cause a domino effect in your community. It's important to be a thought leader on the subject and to help educate your fellow investors.

INVESTOR PERSPECTIVE

Use your manners and make this process more personable and professional. How would you like to be told if you were on the other side of the table? Think ahead to a time when you and the entrepreneur might both be ready to work together on a company. You'd be surprised at the number of deals and entrepreneurs you will see again. It really is a small world. You have to admit, there is something unique about entrepreneurs who continue to chase their dreams and never give up. Who knows, one of those entrepreneurs could be on to something. Never say never.

For the Entrepreneur
Interestingly, most guidebooks for start-ups do not address how to respond and proceed when your deal is declined by an investor. A banker that turns you down will send you an adverse action letter. Angels are encouraged to make things more personable; you never know when you are going to need each other. Make sure to ask the solo angel or angel group how they will be notifying you of a decision and whether you will have the opportunity to remedy the gaps either in the near term or at some future date.

Given that you are coachable and you believe in your company, take the time to fully understand the reasons you have been declined. Without any significant revenue at an early-stage, it is easy for an investor to pick anything that is speculative and claim that it makes the deal too risky. There may be other factors beyond your control. Stay positive.

> **Takeaway**
> Some of the best investment opportunities come from entrepreneurs that you previously passed on. They learn. They refocus. They commit.

29

Be able to close quickly, but don't forget your due diligence

If you're planning to buy a first car for your sixteen year old, you are probably thinking about a used car because of the inevitable accidents. At the dealership, you wouldn't just kick a few tires and say it's fine. You want to take a test drive and do some research to make sure the car is safe and reliable. Well, investing in a start-up or early-stage deal is similar. You want to know what you are buying, and just as importantly, you want to make sure your money is in good hands.

There will be deals that come to you at the eleventh hour from entrepreneurs or other investors. These are deals that are driven by a false urgency to close. You'll want to slow down those deals and analyze the situation. Does the deal conform with your investment objectives, and is it capable of getting to an early exit? You need to show restraint and be the voice of reason regardless of the pressure put on you to close. Don't get bullied; experienced investors will tell you that the odds of failure are much higher if you forego due diligence and ignore your best practices. You need to be better than that.

While investment portfolio allocations, tax deadlines and other factors can accelerate your need to close a deal before you are ready, you should create a set of minimally required procedures that must be checked off before you would ever write a check. You can build a modified version of a Due Diligence Request & Checklist found on various websites including the AngelResourceInstitute.org and 100rules.com. You want to mobilize quickly yet maintain the rigor of risk analysis you conduct on a normal timeline. Can you tap someone knowledgeable in your network in order to become even more comfortable with the industry? Can you prompt several reliable, yet less active angels you know to step in and help with reference checks? Will the founder and the management team be available over the next few days to allow for an accelerated due diligence timeline? A shorter opportunity window for a deal will validate your agility and the strength of your resources and network. It will be challenging. This is where your gut feel really comes into play. If you aren't comfortable, walk away and start looking at your next deal. There is always another opportunity! No lemons.

For the Entrepreneur

You've been told by an angel group that it takes at least ten weeks to obtain funding, sometimes longer. You know by reputation they're never in a hurry to fund anyone. You're still in the screening phase and everyone on your management team is focused on operational issues and revenue. You book a flight to attend a week-long industry conference in order to demo the product.

What happens if the angel group suddenly wants to accelerate due diligence and possibly close quickly?

To hesitate will immediately eliminate you from consideration. This is why nobody on your team should ever be on complete stand-down (or vacation) when you are dealing with an angel group. You'll want a deep bench to cover for times when you're not available. You might want to cancel that industry event or fly back early. This fire-drill could be just another test by the investors. Regardless, it doesn't really matter; you need to be flexible and willing to do whatever it takes to get a deal done.

> **Takeaway**
> Most deals will take sixty to one-hundred-and-twenty days to complete. Anything quicker than that will require all hands on deck.

30

Trust but verify: Sharing due diligence can be a great idea

Politics aside, if someone has nuclear warheads pointed at your head, you're definitely going to want to verify that the missiles have been disarmed before you point your own somewhere else. Don't get caught relying on what someone says; check and double-check that the information is correct. In terms of investing, due diligence resides at the core of angel investing, yet most individual angels do not have the bandwidth or ability to conduct a thorough due diligence on even an early-stage company. You're not just verifying multiple aspects of the product, the market, and the team; you're testing and re-testing the assumptions and conclusions the founder has proposed. At another level, due diligence is a means for you to think and strategize about capital deployment, growth and the most likely path to an acquisition of the business. Plus, your personal due diligence allows you to compare one particular company in the overall context of your deal flow against your current portfolio. For an inexperienced angel investor, leveraging the experience of more experienced investors will reduce risk; however, if you are one of the more experienced investors, are you sure the areas of due diligence that you did not review were conducted appropriately by your syndication partners? Did the risk just increase as a result?

Remember how you want to avoid "divorcing" a portfolio company? Due-diligence is like the "dating" period; you're dating both the company and the potential co-investors.

Regardless of the risk, we say "share." Open your due diligence to other angels and, if you're in an angel group, find other angel groups and co-investors to help you. This not only creates the bandwidth you'll need, it creates operational efficiencies, common standards and an ability to accelerate a decision on a deal if the opportunity arises. Remember that organized, formal angel investing is a fairly new kind of management skill. Sharing company due diligence means that you build a test-bed for solving common problems and you refine best practices as they emerge.

We also like how the discipline of shared due diligence creates a platform for collaborative board monitoring and syndication. When you trust another angel or group to "have your back" on a deal, you are one step closer to the foundational reliance for doing deals together and spreading the risk. Having a larger group also builds the network of potential board members with specific industry experience that will help get the company to an exit. Getting into a deal with people you trust will help sell the deal.

For the Entrepreneur
Self-examination is difficult; yet a thorough outside verification of an opportunity can be extremely insightful for company founders and leaders, especially for start-up entrepreneurs who are passionate and creative by nature but perceive statistical analysis and risk assessment as stifling. The risk of growing a company that will be acquired at a multiple of revenue later on requires a balanced approach.

An angel investor can provide objectivity combined with a level of business experience you may not possess. A group of angel investors can provide an exponential level of objectivity and business insight. If you're going to devote all your energy and time to a company for the next three, five or seven years, it's better to have 15 experienced business professionals look at your deal than one or two. Angels are looking for coachability. Demonstrate that you understand the value of group due diligence and how it makes the deal less risky for all parties. You need to make sure you are consistent; investors will play good cop and bad cop to verify your answers.

Takeaway
Investors must use some level of caution when sharing due diligence. There may be some liability if a portion of the due diligence is incorrect and the other investor groups relied on your statements. Don't take any shortcuts.

31

Never make an emotional investment; you'll lose every time

There's too much at stake to take an emotional approach to early-stage investing. The statistics of failure are sobering. Just liking a concept, an entrepreneur, or a fast-growing market will not get you to a positive exit. With over half of angel deals in the traditional areas of biotech/healthcare and software, you will have the chance to interact with some pretty "cool" products that are based on cutting-edge sciences. As you build your deal flow, you will be inundated with hundreds of science projects that may be that elusive cure to a devastating disease; unfortunately, most will never make it out of the lab because the science, while promising, didn't work. You will want to believe, but be extremely cautious.

One of your roles as an angel is to remove as much emotion as you can from the deal. Start by thinking and planning using objective measures: tables, charts, numerical lists, and your due diligence checklist. Let the entrepreneur wow the audience with his slide decks and slick graphics; you need to stay level headed in order to conduct meaningful and documented due diligence. If you don't, your emotions, and potentially your gut feel, may get in the way. Consider using scoring sheets for screening and due diligence. By summarizing the findings in a succinct manner, you can easily track and compare similar deals to make sure you are doing a complete analysis on the science, intellectual property, sales cycle, market, competition, team, and exit potential. As you know, most start-ups won't be perfect. In fact, most will have defects that need to be addressed. The trick is to balance the good with the bad and to manage the issues that can be abated.

A reliance on accepted metrics creates one version of the truth and gives you, as an investor, one more decision point that takes out the emotions of the deal. Having standard reports and a consistent methodology for board involvement and monitoring keeps everyone focused and using a common framework. Use all the information at your discretion and use it to make a go or no go decision on the investment opportunity. Now, if you could only get all of your portfolio companies to a 10x return. That would really be something to be emotional about.

You can predict what sort of emotional impact a product or service would have on the general public as one of the intangibles of the business, but don't let it have that same impact on your investing.

For the Entrepreneur

You're passionate about your company and its potential. Your energy and enthusiasm are door openers. You have no interest in a corporate job or starting a lifestyle business that has no growth potential. You have the ability to attract like-minded professionals to your management team and your enthusiasm will attract future customers, employees and the media.

These core attributes will be attractive to angel investors, but they can also get you into a lot of trouble quickly if you rely on them completely. The investors on the other side of the table need to take emotion out of deals. They speak of calculated risks and allocating percentages across portfolios. They use scoring tools, metrics and monitoring methodologies to ensure an exit instead of a long-term hold strategy. These rational, organized and quantitative skill-sets and tools could easily clash with your qualitative skills. The strongest deals blend both sets of strengths.

Takeaway
Remove as much emotion as you can from all the deals you see. It's easy to want to invest in every deal that claims to cure lung cancer, especially if you had a loved one die from this illness; unfortunately, if you aren't a multi-billionaire, there is no way you can fund all of them.

32

Don't overpay. If another group jumps in with a bigger offer, it's okay to pass

If we assume that there are over eight hundred thousand new companies started each year in the United States, and approximately fifty thousand of those receive some type of angel funding, it is important to figure out what makes one deal more fundable than the next. But truthfully, of those fifty thousand new deals, probably forty thousand should never have been funded in the first place. Why? Because the deal never stood a chance to start with: the entrepreneur and investor failed to plan for the level of funding needed to succeed, the investor failed to perform due diligence on the market, maybe it was actually a lifestyle business that had no chance of exiting, and so on. An investor can easily find a reason not to fund a company or opportunity. However, with that said, there's typically enough overall deal flow volume to thoughtfully select those opportunities that match up with your expertise and interests without overpaying for the privilege. If you are networked with other angel groups or have been syndicating actively for a couple of months, you are going to see your fair share of good deals.

Don't overpay because you believe you will be missing out on an opportunity or because you have allowed the founder to think he can shop the deal and get someone else to pay more. It's important to remember that once you have completed due diligence and negotiated terms, the valuation on the deal is set. Do not allow it to increase because another funding group or investor gets involved at the eleventh hour. Don't let an inexperienced founder play this game with your time and money. It shows where the entrepreneur's focus is, on his own wallet. Remember, you want the entrepreneur focused on the wealth created at the time of an exit and not before.

It's okay to say no. It's okay to pass when it looks like the valuation is skyrocketing or out of whack. Trust your gut and walk away from a deal where the founder doesn't understand how value is created in early-stage companies. Let another group take the risk and move on to looking at the next batch of deals. Deals are out there and there will always be another opportunity.

As a point of caution, many investors who don't live in California will, from time-to-time, see a couple of deals with higher than normal valuations coming from Silicon Valley and looking for money from you. Be wary of these deals. It could mean that the deals just aren't strong enough to command the higher valuations expected by the entrepreneur or the technology is not as strong, and therefore didn't receive funding from west coast angels, groups or funds there. In all likelihood you will want to pass also. Don't get fooled by the idea. There are better ways to invest in a west coast deal; think syndication and start building your network.

For the Entrepreneur

If you try to force an angel to pay more for your company or you attempt to bring in another group to raise your valuation after you already accepted a term sheet, you will get burned. If for some reason the investor does overpay, he will be irritated with you. He will not respect you or trust you. He will certainly not be as helpful with expertise, contacts or resources as the company grows. He'll be looking to part ways with you soon. And by parting ways, it means finding a way to remove you from the company that you started.

There's not always more money out there. The term sheet you have in hand could be the best it's going to be for now. The more sophisticated angels that can give you the most support along the growth curve and highest chance of an exit are going to pass if you try to drive the company's pre-money valuation higher. Understand that angels have access to hundreds or even thousands of deals each year. They don't need to invest in your company.

Takeaway
Unsophisticated investors often wait on the sidelines for a deal and then trump it because they want in. To keep this from happening, many investors will implement a no-shop clause in their initial term sheets. If you stay in this business long enough, you will see companies take the higher dollars from less sophisticated investors and undervalue the intangible items sophisticated investors bring to a business, such as coaching, networking and access to experts in their industry.

33

Be patient, it's your money

Much of the value you add to a start-up comes from your ability to be patient, to ask questions that don't have quick answers, and to have the discipline to hold back when a deal just doesn't feel right. Trust your gut when you hear that first elevator pitch and pass. Wait until you have an ideal co-investor, syndicate partner or independent board member in place, and do not feel completely rushed to close. Have the fortitude to walk-away and let another angel group fund a deal you really liked at a much higher price than you were willing to pay.

The relationship between angel and founder develops a creative tension where the founder's drive is tempered by the angel's discipline. The result is a more refined business, designed to create value all the way through an exit. If the founder truly understands the non-monetary resources investors, meaning you, bring to the table (expertise, contacts, insight), then patience becomes a key value driver. As an accredited investor, you not only have the gold that the founder does not have (yet), you have the financial framework to understand risk and mitigation and an ability to tap the collective wisdom of your fellow investors.

Don't jump into a deal for the sake of a deal. As an individual investor, you need to make tactical decisions about your portfolio. You have to weigh being patient against having the flexibility to move quickly if you believe it is necessary to optimize an opportunity that may lead to a quick exit with single or low double-digit multiples. Unfortunately, you don't have hundreds of millions of dollars to invest. You need to stay focused and make sure you preserve your funds for the right deals with the right entrepreneurs and right co-investors. Remember, your timeline for an investment is at your discretion. If you don't like something about a deal or the entrepreneur is trying to use schemes to get you to invest before you are ready, you can always walk away and move on. It's your checkbook; make the entrepreneur work for it.

For the Entrepreneur

Angels are essential to the success of a start-up. Once you've exhausted the resources of family and friends, there is no other category of investor better for you than angels, certainly not venture capitalists or bankers. While you may feel frustrated by your options, the unique attributes of angels, especially when they are investing together in a syndicate, more than make up for the amount of time spent chasing money.

While you might be ready to "seize the day," you may feel that the angels you encounter are taking too much time to consider your initial pitch, to conduct due diligence, or to assemble the right board members. Remember that angels are more closely aligned with your interests than you realize; they represent the ideal gauge and feedback loop. If they are cautious, pay attention and understand why. If they offer suggestions for improvement, take them seriously, try them out and report the results. Their feedback could be more valuable than the money they invest.

Takeaway
Patience is a key asset to being an angel investor. If there's anything that you don't like about a deal that's in front of you, you can afford to wait until you find a deal and a team you really like. Find the right deal, with the right entrepreneur and the right idea, before you invest.

34

Know when to walk away. You can't save every deal

You are not a shepherd. You're not responsible for tending to, feeding, or guarding your flock. Portfolio companies are not sheep; you don't need to save every one from falling over the cliff. Yes, your decision to add or not add more money into an existing deal may decide the fate of the company, but you need to be smart about your money. Don't just write a check because everyone else in the deal is investing. This is especially true at the last hour when there might be intense pressure from other investors or the founder to save the company and keep it from going under. Emotions and egos will get in the way of common sense. You may even feel like the other investors or the founder are going rogue on you and things are getting out of control. If so, just walk away. You don't want to throw good money after bad.

You should look at every funding round as an entirely new investment. Even within the same company, treat each deal separately. You have a lot more information now than when you first encountered the company and that can be valuable insight. It may be that everyone around the table thinks he has to invest to keep the company from failing. Failures will happen. That's why you need to diversify your portfolio with multiple investments.

One exception to the rule is "pay to play." This term, if included in deal documents, will force you to invest your allocated amount in the next round of funding in order to maintain your ownership percentage and preserve your share preference. If you decide not to invest, which may be based on your personal finances or the company's performance and outlook, the pay to play provision may convert your equity to common shares and you may become heavily diluted, if not wiped out altogether. There's a lot of pressure on investors when pay to play is included in the closing documents. Again, you don't have to invest; still be sure to treat it as a new deal but with consequences.

With a portfolio of investments, look at your allocation strategy and all the companies where you may be asked or required to put in more money in follow-on rounds. You may not have the deep pockets to protect every bet, especially if there are follow-on rounds or pay-to-play requirements. Sometimes it's okay to walk away from your investment or the deal altogether.

For the Entrepreneur

Don't be surprised if your investors cut you loose with little warning. If your company hits a stretch of losses, your investors may not be willing or able to cover for you. Be very careful when you ask for more capital after all the dry powder has been consumed. This means a new round of funding which will be viewed as a separate investment by most sophisticated investors. You can't really threaten them with the ultimatum that the company will go out of business. If it's not going to be worth the risk, they will walk away. If they do agree to fund, your ownership percentage will be further diluted because you are coming to them from a point of weakness.

This is where communicating and working with your board is so critical. You may be able to detect problems or threats to the business far in advance. You might be able to halt the problems before more capital is required. Investors will have failures in their portfolio; try not to make it your company.

Definition of Pay-to-play
A requirement in some venture capital and angel investments. If a preferred shareholder desires to maintain certain rights as a preferred stockholder, he must participate and invest pro rata in future financings or lose those rights.

35

Don't invest in deals with ten-year exits

Time is not on your side. As soon as you see or hear about a potential deal that projects a ten-year time to exit, think twenty years. It really does take twice as long to exit, given unknown factors and variables that delay or even halt the development of an early-stage company. You don't have the patience, deep capital reserves or liquidity to hang on for that long. Leave those deals to the venture capitalists who play with other people's money.

Most angels are not looking for deals that will need to be taken public via an Initial Public Offering (IPO). That model requires longer hold periods and the likelihood of ever getting to that point is extremely low. You want a quick exit and should be willing to take a lower multiple if a deal has a positive liquidation event in three to five years. You're in this game to take advantage of start-up opportunities. The world changes quickly and requires a lot of portfolio diversification; having your personal funds tied up for a decade means you're not able to take advantage of the next wave of deals and technology companies.

So what are the exceptions to this rule? Certain life sciences deals do require a longer investment timeline because of the long periods of time for clinical development to prove efficacy, safety and mass production of a biologic product; but those are not necessarily matched to the active involvement most angels want in their portfolio companies. A life sciences deal is often binary: the therapeutic either works or it doesn't. In other words, your investment is either a homerun or a strikeout. But as an angel, do you really have the resources necessary to take a life science deal to an exit? You probably do not. If you make a conscious decision to play in this space, you will need to know that your ownership percentage will be seriously diluted over the next thirty plus investment rounds that will be required to get the company through the clinical trials. The best solution is to get involved with an angel group who has expertise and experience investing in this space; otherwise, you could lose a lot of money very, very slowly.

As an angel investor, you need to let the venture capitalists hang around for the higher multiples. If you really like the deal and have expertise in the industry, then determine where you can add value over a shorter time horizon of three to five years. Negotiate very strong terms in your favor if it is anticipated that a venture capital fund will be taking over and holding the cards until the exit. If the founder won't budge, it's okay to walk away from the deal.

For the Entrepreneur

Unlike venture capitalists who invest funds from large institutional partners for long periods of time to achieve high multiples, angels who invest their own personal funds are looking for a much quicker exit. Even in a life sciences deal, which may take twelve to fourteen years to bring a therapeutic product to market, the angel time horizon will be defined and aligned to invest where angels can add value.

Generally, with so many unknown factors and unforeseen events awaiting an early-stage company, it takes two to three times longer to get to an exit than most founders provide for in their business plan. Investors know this intrinsically when funding a deal. Many times the founder will misjudge the receptivity of the market to the product, and more education of potential customers will be needed before they consider buying. Or, the loss of key personnel or the emergence of new or substitute competition can also distract and delay the original timeline. Start-ups will need more time and more money to get to the finish line. Work with your investors and create a strategy with major inflection points and milestones to keep the company on-track.

Takeaway
Capital Reserves
Angels have a finite amount of money to allocate to early-stage investments (typically 5% of net worth.) Angels need their portfolio companies to exit, profitably, in order to keep playing in this space. Don't invest all of your early-stage investable dollars in only one deal; the risks are way too high.

36

Always expect a 10x return or you'll lose the war and be out of the game

If you run out of bullets in a battle, or in the case of investing, run out of money, the war is over. You need to make sure that you maximize the returns on your existing deals so you can constantly add new companies to your portfolio. First, as is the case on all deals, you want to be focused on a strategic exit with a shorter investment timeline. Secondly, you want a strong board team in place that works well with, but also isn't a rubber stamp for, the founder. Finally, a deal must be capable of returning a minimum of 10x, or over time your funds will dry up. If you go into deals only expecting a 3x return, you're wasting your time and money. Remember, most start-ups have the potential for unequivocal failure.

As a rule, things never go as well, or along the path, that founders say they will, especially those who have never started, managed or exited a start-up previously. There are too many variables. When things go wrong, and they will, there are no grace periods. Start-ups can be flawed by market timing alone, either undercapitalized to capture a first mover advantage as a market leader, or overcapitalized for diminishing opportunities that are quickly seized by other start-ups or technologies no one knew about.

So, how do you relate this concept to portfolio strategy? Let's say you have ten investments and you know that, based on history and past performance, half are going to fail to return your original investment. Of these investments, you funded opportunities in markets that only had a maximum upside of a 3x return; you aimed consistently low across your portfolio. On average, even if half of the investments somehow succeeded in giving you a 3x return on five of the ten companies, you need to account for the other five failing and providing no return. Ultimately, your portfolio will give you a 1.5x return on your money over the course of your investments (typically ten years), or an internal rate of return of less than 5%. That's abysmal, given the risk. And remember, this is assuming you hit the maximum on five of the ten investments, which would never happen.

You need to find and fund deals that have much higher potential so you can get a homerun or two in your portfolio. Without these, your returns will be mediocre at best. You might as well consider staying in the stock market or even the bond market; your returns are much safer and your investments are liquid. You want to have high hopes, but unless you get lucky backing another Facebook or Instagram, the best angel strategy is to get in with expectations of a 10x or more return and get out with a 5x to 7x return on the winners. It's still something impressive to talk about with your friends.

For the Entrepreneur

You are not the only company the angel will be backing. You will be part of a portfolio of early-stage investments, and that portfolio is only a small part of that accredited investor's net worth. The portion of net worth that angels put at risk requires that they seek much higher multiples than they might see through other investment classes, such as real estate, bonds, or stock investments in public equities as represented by the S&P 500 or NASDAQ.

While you don't have to reach for the high bar required by venture capitalists of a 30x return, you should be very comfortable understanding how your company will provide investors at least a 10x return over a shorter time period. Conveniently, when angels get involved in their deals, they leverage their resources and network to help a company exit at higher multiples.

Takeaway
Spread your risk and your money. Portfolio diversification is extremely important to the success of an investor. One deal, one investment, one failure, and you're out of the game. To achieve your return on investment, your portfolio must have at least ten deals.

37

Don't invest in deals that you can't explain to your spouse

You may have a deal that really strikes you or, you've come across a strong, reliable founder you'd really like to work with over the course of several years to launch a company and to take it to an exit. Even your fellow investors like the deal and the management team, and everything has gone smoothly through screening and due diligence. You've networked and found the ideal independent board member to reduce the risk even more.

The question remains, can you explain the deal to your spouse in a clear manner so that he or she understands it in a reasonable amount of time for the subject matter? If not, you may have an early sign of how receptive the market could be to the new concept or technology. Some deals are so innovative and ahead of their time, they haven't developed the simplicity and ease of articulation that we associate with more established technologies. There was a time when the concept of a "personal computer" was something most people would have a difficult time grasping. Think about how you might have described a smart phone 30 years ago: you mean your telephone has detailed street maps in it, is not tethered securely to the wall and takes home movies?

There's a difference between a person not being able to understand what something is or what it does, and wanting to use it or understanding why it exists. Twitter is a good example. Easy to explain, but harder to explain "why" anyone would want to use it before everyone did just that!

Involving your family in your investing process reduces risk. A spouse's insight at this point may be invaluable. Not only are you introducing a more impartial form of analysis and scrutiny to the formal angel process, you're giving your family exposure to the fun of being an angel investor.

This exercise is also helpful if there are any consumer products or services involved. Would your spouse buy it? Would she or he recommend it to their friends and colleagues? Perhaps your spouse also has a business background, which could be helpful for business-to-business deals that you are considering. If you can't explain what a company does, especially to your family and friends in layman terms, do you really want to be in the deal?

For the Entrepreneur

It's easy, when hunting money, to think of angels in relative isolation. Perhaps you've met an angel at a business networking event or through your attorney. Just remember the good ones are incredibly resourceful. They rely on a wide network of contacts to help them thoroughly understand deals and judge the likelihood of an exit.

Just as we encourage the angels to explain your deal to a spouse or other family members, there's no reason you shouldn't do the same. Make sure your family understands exactly what you are doing. Can they spout your elevator pitch verbatim to anyone who asks?

This rule also argues strongly for your ability to articulate the deal, the market opportunity and technology in very simple terms. As you craft your elevator pitch, ask yourself: can the angel investors I present this to explain it to their spouses in such a way that is clear? If not, investors may forget about you.

Takeaway
Consider joining an angel group and attending meetings as a family. The best groups (successful and fun) have significant gender and age diversity at meetings.

38

Valuation is not a science, it is a negotiation

We recommend angels spend more time learning how to syndicate and exit, and less time perfecting pre-money valuations. Valuation is not a science; it's part of the negotiation process between the angel and the entrepreneur. Your time is better spent going over what it will take to get a solid return at the time of the exit than giving a reality check to the entrepreneur about what the company is really worth at the time of investment. Sometimes the entrepreneur gets hung up on the up-front value and forgets about the wealth that is created at the exit. If founders will keep valuations low, and be in a position to get a strong investment from a syndicate of angels, they could become very wealthy once they hit their milestones and get to a liquidation event. Every deal has to be capable of providing a large enough multiple to offset the risk of investing in start-up deals.

Early-stage investor and author Basil Peters who, in his book, "Early Exits," asked the question and conducted the research: how many companies out there actually sell for $100 million? The answer is not that many. Most transactions are under $20 million. So, how can an entrepreneur assign a $5 million pre-money valuation to a company and still get the returns required for investors? For an angel to put $4 million into the deal and get the 10x returns that are needed to account for the risk, it's difficult to see how that will happen if the exit is going to be $20 million or less. In this scenario, a $4 million investment with a $5 million pre-money would create a $9 million post-valuation deal. A 10x return would need a $90 million exit, assuming no additional funding rounds are required. It just doesn't happen very often.

Speaking of additional funding rounds, it is imperative to know how dilution impacts a deal and how it relates to the initial pre-money valuation. As an investor, you should have an idea of the future funding needs for every deal and use that to calculate how dilution may impact your ownership position. While you don't want to set a valuation that significantly dilutes the previous investors and even the entrepreneur, you need to make sure that if you invest you will get your required returns. You want a valuation that allows you to do the deal with angel money only and doesn't need venture capital money. And, if you know additional funds will be required, you and your co-investors should have enough dry powder allocated for that. Otherwise, you should consider walking away from the deal before making your first investment.

Some entrepreneurs will get it and understand that the lower valuation helps get everyone involved to a positive exit. What happens when you set a valuation and the entrepreneur is not happy with it but takes it anyway? Do you really want to be in that deal with that founder for five or ten years? Walk away!

For the Entrepreneur

Here are four valuation methods you should definitely *not* use or rely upon when negotiating with an individual angel investor or an angel group:

1. The Founder Multiple: My company is worth $1 million for every founder that we have listed on the capitalization table.

2. Comparables: My company is worth $7 million pre-money because another angel-backed start-up that develops a similar kind of technology just sold for that amount and we are better.

3. Grants: My company received $9 million in grant money, so my company is worth at least that amount.

4. The Top-Down Pie Slice: The overall market is currently $1 billion and growing quickly. If we only capture one-half of one percent of this market, even estimating conservatively at 1x annual revenue, we are worth $5 million.

> **Takeaway**
> For a full review of valuation methods used by angels, including the one commonly used by venture capitalists, please visit 100rules.com.

39

A company is only worth what someone is willing to pay

During the stage of negotiating the terms and value of a particular start-up, we think there is far too much emphasis on specific valuation. From the premise of exit-designed investing, this is missing the point. Absent the founder's exuberance and the levels of noise in that specific industry, exits remain sobering. Based on past data, half of all early-stage deals will probably fail. What does that mean? It means that half of the deals in your angel portfolio could be worthless.

What a founder claims the company is worth, no matter the source, is not relevant to your objectives. Multiples of projected revenue, comparable companies, or similarities to other technologies don't really matter. What really matters is what could the mature company be worth at the time of exit, if we get involved as angels? How much are we willing to invest now based on assumptions? What matters to both you and the investor is how the valuation now will affect the payoff at exit.

A founder's extreme obsession with the valuation of his company could be seen as a negative attribute. The more assertive or defensive the founder is about the exact value of the company before you invest, the more that should spur you to greater scrutiny, to make sure that information, material to the deal, is neither being withheld or manipulated.

A founder who is focused on a somewhat arbitrary number is one who may not thoroughly understand the added value that angel investors bring to early-stage companies. Does the founder understand what the investor and board members represent in terms of business and industry knowledge? Does the founder understand the lack of expertise and depth of the management team? Does the founder understand that ultimately it will not be the buzz around the technology, the trademarked logos or even company revenue that will induce a strategic acquirer to pull the trigger on a deal? As the investor, remember that the entrepreneur does not set the terms or value of the deal, you do!

For the Entrepreneur

In the simplest form of valuation, your company is worth exactly what someone else is willing to pay for it. And from there it gets complicated. How risky is your business compared to the other investments in the angel's portfolio? Where are you located geographically? How does your industry align with the expertise of the angel and potential board members? What critical events have just happened or will happen soon? A product beta test with a customer can fail, competitors will emerge or a new market opens that no one had originally considered. These are all variables considered in the valuation.

What's ultimately the most important thing for you in an angel funding environment is the exit pathway. Value is created incrementally after the closing through formal board monitoring and informal mentoring, and then dramatically from the ability to identify potential acquirers and close on a strategic exit. Work with your investors on a strategy and make sure you can show them, regardless of the pre-money valuation, how they will get a minimum of a 10x return on their investment.

Takeaway
The more assertive or defensive the founder is about the exact value of the company before you invest, the more that should spur you to greater scrutiny on the deal. The value of an early-stage company is in the eye of the investor. Entrepreneurs estimate and guess. Whatever amount the investor chooses to put into the company, and the amount a buyer is willing to pay to buy the company at the exit, is the ultimate gauge of value.

40

Corporate investors are great, but it doesn't mean the deal is good

The risks are so high with start-ups, it's tempting to rely on a well-known name or corporate brand associated with a deal. Would you invest in a deal just because a Fortune 500 did? As you know, relationships matter tremendously when creating value from an unproven technology or innovative service. Just make sure you understand the level of commitment from the corporate partners and how it aligns with your exit plans.

The structure of the deal is ultimately what matters. Having a recognized corporate supporter could inflate expectations, give a founder false assumptions for reaching milestones, and drive the pre-money valuation beyond where angels are comfortable or what is justified.

Just as you always invest with the exit in mind, you should always start with the premise that the majority of the value you wish to drive doesn't really exist at the beginning. The value created is based on an ability to execute the plan, to insert (and substitute) the right board members at the right time, to line up potential acquirers and to negotiate a sale on a fast timeline with a reasonable rate of return.

You have to remember, large corporate partners have the security of an established brand and deep pockets; and mistakes are easily covered-up by customer loyalty, large profits, or operating divisions that can provide support for each other. Losses in one deal can offset gains from another deal. In a pinch, divisions can be sold and assets can be liquidated. They can also just raise more capital from a comparatively limitless pool.

What could be a solid return for you could also barely move the needle for a corporate investor. As a result, your portfolio company could become a lifestyle business. Think about a scenario where the co-investor, that very same corporate investor, blocks the sale of the portfolio company because they are more interested in keeping it independent. The reason they invested in the first place was to help fund a company that supplies them with goods and services. As the old saying goes, "why buy the cow when you can get the milk for free?"

INVESTOR PERSPECTIVE

Angels, and start-ups, don't have these luxuries or liquidity options. Your capacity to network and mentor could be the subtle factors that result in the exit. You don't have to be strong-armed by a founder wielding star power. You can confidently walk away from a deal where the fundamentals are not in place. Let someone else deal with what could be tremendous potential but more likely pitfalls in this kind of deal.

For the Entrepreneur

You want lift. You want that edge to make your company distinctive when it comes to first round funding. Perhaps your technology has attracted a corporate executive interest or even a seed investment from a well-known brand.

Attaching a high-profile name to a project doesn't necessarily benefit you when it comes to making your way through the deal screening process and into due diligence and funding. It could actually harm you and create friction with angel investors who understand what it takes to reach an exit. There's a significant difference between what it takes to create corporate success and the agility needed to navigate the risky waters of being a start-up. Will your corporate contact truly add value with day-to-day monitoring, mentoring and providing immediate feedback like an angel board member will? You should know that the size of the check shouldn't guarantee current or future board representation. Start-ups need team players who understand early-stage business needs like bootstrapping, building a sales team with little to no money, developing a guerrilla marketing campaign, and finding a quick exit.

> **Takeaway**
> A good deal is more than money and a high-profile investor.

41

Avoid friendly fire: conduct due diligence on your co-investors

While you may be highly focused on the founding team risk and unknowns related to the product and market, don't forget to thoroughly vet your co-investors at the same time. This is an often-overlooked step, but one that you should consider because with shorter exit timelines, you're going to be around your co-investors a lot longer than any company in your portfolio.

Here are some potential areas of exposure. Your co-investors may be from a different part of the country. He may have higher deal flow or see fewer deals. He may be more desperate or guarded in terms of closing the deal. His term sheet may be more restrictive or loose than what you're willing to extend to the founder.

You may be looking to put different amounts of money into the deal. If your co-investors feel that the amount of money invested is what determines the appointment of board members, and you believe it should be more aligned to the knowledge of a specific industry and access to exit partners, then you will have some serious philosophical differences to resolve.

There may be basic trust issues. Will a co-investor side with the founder because of geographic proximity initially, or because over time he likes the deal much more than you do since he is spending more time with it? Will that person encourage side deals, rogue tactics or other behaviors that could put your investment at risk? Does he bring the same business ethics to the table? Does he have dry powder in reserve for the deal?

It's important to do your homework on your co-investors. You can conduct due diligence and solicit feedback from other angel groups or members of the leading national angel association(s) who may have had other dealings with your prospective partners. It's okay to ask questions. Remember, your co-investors will be researching you too! As you vet them, you should determine how they will participate in due diligence, board monitoring and the acquisition (exit) phase. Knowing your partners will not only help you determine if you can work well with them; it will allow you to know their strengths and weaknesses that your skillset may balance.

For the Entrepreneur

When angels band together, or syndicate, you benefit from a greater network of experience, contacts and board representation that matches up with your specific industry and complements the skill sets represented on your management team. It also allows you to have board representation in closer geographic vicinity or with specialized functional skills to help you move forward at a more rapid pace.

If the deal is progressing and there is a syndicate involved, you may find that the angel's attention is temporarily distracted during due diligence because he's verifying that the other investors in the deal are the right fit. It takes time to incorporate new investors into the process. You may need to be extraordinarily patient and cooperative, given the higher number of moving parts in the deal. However, once the deal closes, you should really see the lift of having additional resources at your disposal.

> **Takeaway**
> Trust is a huge part of co-investing. Make sure to protect yourself by understanding your legal responsibilities if you share due diligence reports and/or disclose confidential information.

42

Parking lot deal screening. Know what the founder is driving

You will have several opportunities for the founding team to give you clues about their values, level of focus and an indication of future behavior. It may be the type of car the founder drives to the first meeting, the luxury watch you notice during a presentation, or other examples of high-end purchases at the company's office. These status symbols could be important to how the founder successfully cultivates people and sells, but they're not necessarily appropriate now, especially in a start-up environment. If the amount of money the company is seeking to raise is less than the founder has in his garage on four wheels, that can be a bad sign.

On the opposite side, there are also founders who inappropriately dress like bums because they think that's what a start-up is about. You want to see a founder who dresses professionally but knows how to budget and bootstrap. You'd like to see a company leader who understands the scarcity of cash and the benefits of keeping overhead expenses low. You also want to see personal discipline and focus. Placing emphasis on personal goods and luxuries can be a distraction, and a real lack of financial discipline can put one in personal debt and create all kinds of potential problems for the company. An entrepreneur should be concerned with the company and with his team.

Take a closer look at the capitalization table. What is the founder really bringing to the deal other than the idea, a working prototype and membership at several country clubs? If you detect any kind of ostentatious display, you are free to probe more directly about what other liquid assets the founder may be holding back that should be going into the company. Scrutinize the founder's expectation for compensation and benefits. The founder should be comfortable, but should not be relying on salary to maintain an extravagant lifestyle. Tread carefully: displays of luxury give you the latitude to increase levels of inquiry around personal finances before you proceed to any form of due diligence or negotiation of terms. If the founder is wearing leather driving gloves, he shouldn't necessarily be in the driver's seat.

For the Entrepreneur

With all the risk involved, investors have high sensitivity levels. Your company most likely has not established a track record or booked any revenue from product sales. You and your team are first-timers at running a company. First impressions will matter tremendously. Any display or mention of personal luxury items like cars, watches, expensive clothing or vacations will cause your investor to do a double-take, and they may ask you point-blank how much you are putting into the deal. Money, not time. They may file the observation away for a later discussion.

You want to appear professional and knowledgeable, but hungry. You're willing to defer a large salary and benefit package for a later date because you are focused on building wealth, not a lifestyle. It's mostly about having the discipline to focus on the task at hand and forgo any distractions. Since you're not putting much cash in the deal, you better appear motivated to get your company to an exit.

Takeaway
If the entrepreneur drives a Jaguar to the first meeting, it's okay to ask if he is making a sizable "cash" investment in the company, too.

43

Do background checks on the entire management team

Did you know you're issued a trench coat and magnifying glass when you become an angel? You're not just an investor; you're a private detective, an investigator. A portion of your personal wealth is on the line, and chances are little to none of finding the founder's own personal cash on the capitalization table.

Start every deal by being suspicious. Treat each entrepreneur with absolute respect but proceed with caution. After you ask a probing question, don't settle; probe further and approach all aspects of the deal from different angles. See if you can uncover areas of weakness now, before you invest money and expose your valued network of contacts to the founder and the management team. You can be faulted for your scrutiny, but if it keeps you from being the proverbial "sucker born every minute," it is worth the risk.

If the deal blows up, it only hastened something that would have most likely happened to half your investments anyway. The good news is that you avoided losing money in this deal. Even if it puts a temporary pinch in your deal flow and efforts to create a diverse portfolio, intense background checks for everyone on the team are a key tactic. You're not just looking for outright fraud. You might be on the lookout for subtle signs of tension, of fudging and obfuscation. If there's a problem, there's probably a fresh trail somewhere.

Of course, the founder will give you glowing references. You should accept them as a starting point, but ask for other references on the spot. See how the founder reacts. A cooperative founder understands the importance of your scrutiny and will be helpful. A potential problem founder might become defensive, or try to change the subject. Do you really want to tolerate that kind of behavior for the next three to five to ten years, assuming things go well? You can also conduct background checks on the references themselves. There's nothing wrong with going beyond what is given to you at face value. Sherlock Holmes probably could have been a great investor!

For the Entrepreneur

You may be confident in your own personal and professional reputation, but will the rest of your management team hold up to the scrutiny of an intense background check by a committee of angels? Will the references you provide hold up to the heat?

In today's internet search and social media environment, reputation management is essential. Angels are not only looking for overt fraud. They're looking for tendencies and hints of potential malfeasance. Stress changes everything. Angels are looking preemptively for risks that could derail the deal the closer it gets to exit. You don't want the downfall to be an internally-generated factor linked to the team you assembled.

You should conduct your own form of due diligence, especially on members of your management team with equity on the capitalization table. Now is the time to prepare and invest in some serious scrutiny of your own team. Find the pitfalls before your potential investors find them.

Takeaway
Attorneys are excellent resources for conducting background checks. Check the Angel Capital Association's website for a full list of low-cost providers. If you find that the entrepreneur failed in a previous start-up or even had to file for bankruptcy, remember, it's part of the game. What's important is that they disclosed it to you.

44

Partner with other investors to conduct due diligence

Due diligence is complicated and challenging. You must simultaneously analyze an industry, thoroughly vet a management team and verify all elements of the proposed business plan. Even small tasks matter, like double-checking the founder's math and scrutinizing the authenticity of the references you've been given. There will also be site visits and any number of meetings that are postponed or rescheduled.

If things are progressing well with the deal, you'll be considering how this particular deal fits with your portfolio diversification strategy and how risks will be balanced. If you will not be serving in a board capacity, you'll be thinking ahead and considering a list of strong board members for the deal. You may need to search, identify and secure a commitment from a potential independent board member with specific industry experience to make you more comfortable with the investment.

Conducting due diligence on your own can be very difficult. You're not just checking specific facts and broader representations about technologies and markets; you're also vetting personal characteristics of the founding team, such as integrity, passion, flexibility, energy and overall leadership, and a deep personal drive to see things through to an exit.

This is why having an angel fund or group makes so much sense. You can not only spread the workload, you can attack these significant tasks according to specialties. That creates much greater efficiency, both for you as an angel and for the entrepreneur who is waiting for clear direction. The more intense levels of due diligence benefit the founder tremendously. It creates an environment for open communication and consistent monitoring that improves the chance of a quick exit. Given the risk and the ability to add value at the very early stages, it makes sense to bring as many resources to the table as possible. Bring in the support of other co-investors in a syndicate as soon as you can. While you can have too many people conducting due diligence at the same time, it beats not having enough people.

For the Entrepreneur

Due diligence is not something to merely endure before you get the money. If your deal was less than promising, you would have been politely eliminated at the screening round. Due diligence is foundational to an investor's ability to add value. It is time-consuming, detailed, stressful and thorough because it is exit-focused. "Measure twice, cut once," as they say.

If you're dealing with a single angel investor, understand the complexity of the undertaking. Be as cooperative and forthright as possible. If you're dealing with an angel fund or organized group, view that as the highest compliment. A team of experienced business people believe in you and plan to back you for up to five or ten years with their best resources. It is in your best interest to view yourself as part of the due diligence and to provide the best information in a timely manner.

Takeaway
Entrepreneurs should have due diligence materials prepared for investors before they start seeking money. Angels are busy and their attention spans are short. If an entrepreneur delays getting the materials, investors may move on from the deal. Make sure to have a common due diligence checklist available for entrepreneurs and all investors to review.

45

Creating incentives for entrepreneurs will align interests with investors

Before you ever invest a dollar into an early-stage deal, you need to make sure that your plans for the company match the plans of the founder who will, more than likely, own the largest share of the company's stock. Does the founder agree that he will make his fortune when the company is sold, and not by collecting a salary? Does the founder want to sell at all, or is he emotionally attached to the company more so than the potential money it can create? If you are satisfied with the answers, you want to proactively put the right incentives in place, at the time of funding, to motivate the founder to get to a quick exit rather than trying to create incentives retroactively. By then it could be too late. You'll want to have incentives designed to motivate a founder when stress levels are expected to increase dramatically. Think exits. Some founders have a tendency to lose their bearings in the face of selling their company or regretting things that might have transpired differently.

For the most part, you want to rely on positive incentives for the founder; focus on the carrots, rather than the sticks. You need to be able to show that, with angel-only funding, the original equity is not overly diluted. If a founder works cooperatively with you toward an acquisition, remains coachable and open to board guidance, he'll have a much greater chance of selling the company with a strong exit instead of needing a venture capitalist to come in with a potentially devastating cram-down and years of additional operations. A VC investment will, most likely, dilute the founder's equity stake and create a more unstable, top-down controlling environment that may also lead to the entrepreneur losing his role as the top executive in the company.

As an investor, you will have affirmative and negative covenants in place in the closing documents. These will provide stronger legal incentives and lessen the threat of default. You're an angel investor because of the unique value you can add to both a company and the founder's management abilities, so having a strong board to turn to can be positive incentive for founders.

In addition to supporting the founder, you'll also need a formal incentive plan for the management team. Consider all the possible components, including stock options, profit-sharing and bonuses based on meeting revenue or other mission-critical milestones. In many cases, the exit is not only valued in terms of the business, it is also based on the people involved. Keep the key personnel motivated and incentivized for an exit.

For the Entrepreneur

You've always set personal goals that are achievable due to your strong inner drive. With angel funding, those goals become externalized and driven by exit objectives. Work with your angels to develop equity and compensation incentives for you and your management team.

Here are the payoffs when you are exit-focused. You will no longer be "under the gun." You'll have less chance of burning out by sticking with the company too long. The money you will make with an exit can fund your next company, and you might receive more favorable terms as a successful exited entrepreneur. If you exit, you won't have to worry about your equity share being diluted in the event that venture capital funding is needed. You may be better suited as an early stage CEO, since your skill set and temperament are not as well matched for a diminished role inside a large, bureaucratic corporation. Investors will not have an issue creating incentives for you and your team as long as the payout is connected to a liquidity event that also benefits them.

Takeaway
Always create a management stock option pool when investing and provide incentives for founders to reach an exit, quickly.

46

A deal is a deal... or is it?

Term sheets, like handshakes, are typically non-binding. The presumption is that if you give a founder a term sheet, then you have the capability and expectation to close the deal. There may still be additional back-and-forth negotiation and differences of opinion until the long-form investment document is completed, but your intent is to make the deal happen. The reason for this is that you have spent time and money in the course of due diligence and you wouldn't be extending a term sheet unless you were ready to proceed. You also want to stop the entrepreneur from shopping the deal around to other investors, and you don't want him coming back to you with different terms at a time when you're ready to close because he found an investor willing to pay more.

Help founders understand that part of what can make a deal attractive is not having to spend more time and energy on negotiating the deal than will be spent on running the company. Make sure you are consistent with how you provide term sheets. You may also need to educate founders on the implication of each clause or key concept, as they may not be completely familiar with these terms. Make sure an entrepreneur has an attorney he trusts that has the capability of being a deal-maker instead of a deal-breaker. If not, you may want to recommend an attorney who worked on other deals you were involved with.

The length of a term sheet may vary by area of the country. In some areas you might see a term sheet that is only one page long because there is a lot of experience with and competition for funding start-ups. In the southeast, if an angel or angel group has been burned or hurt by deal terms, you might see a protective 25-page term sheet that covers every possible scenario. If you need a term sheet template for your next deal, they are readily available from national associations like National Venture Capital Association (NVCA) or the Angel Resource Institute (ARI), from law firms that specialize in venture investment, or in the tool section of this book.

Note: Some investor groups prefer to provide a term sheet prior to starting due diligence to set expectations and to ensure that the entrepreneur will agree to terms as set forth. While this practice is acceptable, the likelihood of completing a deal is usually much lower, since neither party truly knows what will be uncovered in the days and weeks ahead.

For the Entrepreneur

Term sheets may vary depending on your region of the country and the experience of your investors. Term sheets are usually non-binding because, when an angel gives you one after several weeks of due diligence, it means you have his trust and he expects to close the deal. It's acceptable to ask the investor: of all the term sheets that you signed, how many of them successfully closed?

If an angel gives you a term sheet right away, he's giving you a roadmap of what to expect. If there are items like obtaining key-man life insurance, you'll know ahead of time what you need to get done before a closing can occur.

If you have a signed term sheet, don't shop it to other groups for better terms. Investors will not like this. However, it's perfectly acceptable to actively search for other investors who may want to co-invest in the deal. Remember, there is a strong possibility that the deal still falls apart in due diligence since the term sheet is non-binding. Some areas of the country, especially in California where there are a significant number of investors, may have a non-shop clause in the term sheet.

> **Definition of Term Sheet**
> A document that outlines the key terms of a proposed transaction. It also provides information that will be used as the basis for the deal documents, including the capitalization table, legal terms and the rights of all parties. The term sheet is typically non-binding, except for certain provisions.

47

If it takes more than three months to conduct due diligence, start over

If you haven't concluded the due diligence of a company in ninety days, start over. The "current financial" statement you've been relying upon will need to be replaced by three months of new activity. There might be significant changes in the two sets of financials, both detrimental and encouraging. The founder may have held back financial information that must now be recognized and analyzed, like a major expense or receivable. Conversely, a key customer might have been signed or a milestone reached in product development during the time you've had the deal under scrutiny.

At ninety days, it's important to find out why due diligence took so long. Did the entrepreneur fail to provide documents on time? Are you not as interested in the deal as you originally thought? Is your syndication not coming together? Regardless of the answers, something is definitely not right. As a result, you should now rethink your portfolio diversification. Times have changed. You may have closed on or exited other deals during this period. The deal you've been analyzing may require new consideration in light of your portfolio balance or the portfolio of your angel fund and syndication partners. There might be changes in the leadership of the deal, and the reset on due diligence needs to align with any new direction that has been set. You also may have missed out on board members you wanted to appoint.

A long due diligence period will place tremendous stress on the founder. He may not have the patience to even wait around, depending on geographical and industry factors. The delay might surface high-pressure tactics and behaviors that were not evident during the screening phase. There may also be reference checks or representations in the original business plan that need to be adjusted. It's also possible that the target market has shifted or that new competitors or technologies have emerged. A critical member of the founding team may have left for a new job. Three months is an extremely long period of time for an early-stage company and in many technology-related industries. Make sure you're respecting the value of your founder's and your co-investors time during due diligence. It's okay to walk away from the deal at any time.

For the Entrepreneur

As someone with a driven personality, it's no fun to wait for an answer. You might find working with an angel or fund frustrating at first. You may have closed quickly when you received informal investments from friends and family at the seed stage, and you probably carried a limited amount of overhead expense. While you may have faster approval from an individual angel, consider the benefits of delays from a group. By sharing due diligence and possibly syndicating with multiple investors, your funding partners are rapidly mitigating risk. They are putting in place board members with industry experience. They are increasing the chances for everyone that there will be an acquisition and exit, instead of running out of cash and going out of business. Conversely, if the group is taking too long to conduct due diligence, you want to be able to move on and seek funding from other sources. If communication with an investor during due diligence suddenly stops, it's probably a bad sign. Do everything you can to keep all of the potential investors engaged during due diligence.

Takeaway
Angels should be able to conduct due diligence in ninety days or less. If not, something's not right with the deal, or the investor is looking at too many deals at one time. Typically, less than 10% of all deals taken to due diligence are funded.

48

Be honest: It's okay to invest in a company that you want to run

Many times, an angel investor sees a business and thinks to themselves, "I would love to run that!" You might see a technology or business model that immediately catches your attention. It may be especially attractive if it is in your industry or fixes a problem in an industry you know well.

You see opportunities in deals where the founders don't have the ability or knowledge to grow past the seed stage. If you leave the key founder in place as CEO, the risk is that it will remain a lifestyle business or will always be four guys locked in a basement perfecting the technology. You may be tempted to inform the founder that he may be replaced in the top job later on in future rounds, so why not step out of the way now and let you run it?

There are ulterior or hidden motives for almost every investment made, and in many cases that motive is that an investor wants the opportunity to run the company at some point. He may have a family member who could run it, or he sees that he can use an existing company he owns as a supplier to the new portfolio company.

Investors need to be forthright about their intentions. If you have a gut feeling you want to run the company, you need to express that interest early and out in the open. You may have other angels or syndicate members who may not want you to run it, and their investments may be contingent on it. Or, on the positive side, the investor group may love if you do. Even if you are the only investor, it's important that you don't write terms into the deal for the sole purpose of taking over once the entrepreneur fails; you will be rooting for failure and not providing the founder with your best efforts. Be fair to the entrepreneur and be fair to yourself.

In the end, the dilemma of who eventually runs the company should be left to the board. The board, with its broader range of expertise, will be focused on putting the best leader in place to give the best possible return to investors. Of course, another solution is to go out and start your own business from scratch… in which case you should spend more time on the "For the Entrepreneur" sections of this book.

For the Entrepreneur

Your start-up may attract more than angel money and board members who want to mentor you. An investor may see a job for himself or a job for a friend or a family member in your company. It won't be a job working for you; he will want your CEO role.

It's important to remember that investors have ownership in all kinds of other companies. An investor may be part of a family business, like a staffing agency or office supply house; as a result, any investment he makes in your deal will be contingent upon using his own company as your main supplier. There are all kinds of hidden motives at play. Be aware of these possibilities when you look for outside funding. Make sure that you have the capability and leadership to take your company all the way to an exit. Do not become complacent just because you are the founder and have majority ownership of the shares. Who knows, maybe you'd like to take a backseat to an investor who is willing to step in and help guide your company toward an exit? It takes a dedicated team to make a company successful, and you could learn a lot from an angel who has done it before.

Takeaway
Investors need to be forthright about their intentions associated with a deal.

49

Have a few relievers in the bullpen; not all entrepreneurs can go the distance

In baseball, starting pitchers don't typically go all nine innings. There are guys who specialize in closing out the game to hold on for the win. Like a game, it's tough for an entrepreneur to have the ability and the energy to take a company from start-up to an exit on his own. Even the five years it takes to reach an early exit can be a long time. Founders can burn out or have unexpected personal conflicts that derail their leadership and vision. Since the goal is the sale of the company, you, as an investor, need to think in objective terms about who will be running the business at each phase of the deal. You'll be conducting the same exercise as a coach or general manager for a baseball team.

As early as the screening phase, you should be analyzing whether the founder has the energy and drive to go the distance. Have direct conversations about this concern, if you have it. Get the opinion of other angels or groups in the syndicate. Many scientific founders and technologists are happiest in a laboratory setting, where they can control all the elements. Not everyone has the personality or business skills to lead at very small and medium-sized business levels. There are, however, exceptions where a genius is also top CEO material.

If you suspect that there will eventually be a need for transition, have a contingency plan in place and be transparent about it. Perhaps in due diligence you have identified a management team member who, with the right mentoring from the board and some additional experience, can step into the lead role in place of the founder. Perhaps one of the board members is best suited to take on the CEO responsibilities. We've noted elsewhere in this book that the period prior to an exit can be an extremely stressful time for a founder at the helm of a company. It's possible that he was able to take you 95% of the way, but that final 5% was just not possible. Be prepared to call somebody else in from the bullpen to maintain your exit trajectory and finish the sale.

For the Entrepreneur

Work with your investment partners during initial discussions and due diligence to anticipate how your leadership role will evolve with the company, from current funding all the way to exit. Are your skills and temperament suited for all stages? If not, can you afford to take the time to learn new business skills on the fly? Should you be thinking about grooming someone from your management team as an understudy, so that there are no hiccups during the later and exit stages of the company?

If your contribution to the value of the company is primarily scientific, technological, or simply based on specialized market knowledge, you should take some time now to honestly assess your ability to lead a management team, to drive the organization to meet operational milestones, and to ramp up sales. Once you take money from the investors, you will have limited flexibility (input) to make changes at the top; it will become a board issue.

Takeaway
If you have the right person in place to lead the company through the exit, but he or she needs help, consider using stock options to give incentives to a board member to act as an Executive Chairman. The chairman will take on some day-to-day responsibilities with the company to fill the gaps.

50

Don't assume a previously successful entrepreneur should be funded again

Past success can breed future success; just don't assume it will. If a founder has a history of success and constantly brags about it to investors, push back and politely ask, "If you have had all this financial success, why do you need my money in your new deal? Why don't you fund it yourself?"

The answer is going to be telling. If that founder plans on co-investing and is using additional funds to ramp up the company quicker to meet market needs, then we are good-to-go. However, if the answer is that the entrepreneur is illiquid or doesn't like the stress of having too much at stake, then it may be time to walk. Often, with semi-successful entrepreneurs, their ego is too big and their financial commitment is too small.

Remember, every deal is different. This applies to entrepreneurs as well as investors. Entrepreneurs with failures can be funded if they learned valuable lessons along the way and are open to coaching and board monitoring on the next deal. A successful entrepreneur may not have learned very much with that first win and he assumes every deal will go the same way. He may have hit the right market at the right time on that first success and believes he can repeat easily the second time around.

As a private investor, you are completely within reason to ask an entrepreneur about his personal finances and willingness to co-invest with you in the deal. You're also free to probe any reluctance he may have to putting in money. If the entrepreneur is riding on previous success and looking only for your money, you might be better off looking at other deals.

For the Entrepreneur
Beware of success. You may not learn enough from it to be valuable to investors. Was your past win truly because of your brilliance and leadership, or can you attribute some of it to other factors such as market timing, the right mix of customers early on, larger economic forces beyond your personal control, or just plain luck?

If you've been fortunate to take your idea all the way to an exit previously, and have generated some personal wealth, be prepared to put some of that money at risk in your next deal. Be prepared for increased investor scrutiny. Don't expect investors to invest blindly or give you preferential terms because of your achievement.

Now that you've been successful, you should conduct due diligence on your own deal before you take it to an investor. Is this the right product for this market at this point in time? Should I keep the same management team as before, or should I bring in other talent to match the unique attributes of this new deal?

Takeaway
A successful entrepreneur who doesn't want to co-invest his own wealth in future deals is not only asking investors to take on too much risk, he's probably not very coachable or open to board monitoring either. Seriously think about walking away.

51

Investing in a company with a "brand name" CEO isn't always good

Beware of the founder who already had a successful exit. You'll probably hear him before he actually arrives. If he's constantly referring to "my last company", then you should be extra diligent. Even with the exact same management team, the execution variables are different with a new company. Money and success will change each team member's motivation. Is everyone equally hungry this time around?

You may be proceeding with caution, but you might also be strong-armed by another investor or angel group that wants to fund the deal based solely on the CEO's track record. Trust your gut. Get underneath the hood and look at the timing belt. Does a success over the past five years mean anything in this particular industry over the next five years? Has the industry over-heated? Have the exits attracted hype and higher valuations?

Where you might really see a difference is in the deal terms and valuations. An emboldened, successful CEO will tend to play more investors against one another to drive up pre-money valuations and loosen up term sheets. This can be especially true in areas of the country that lack many serial entrepreneurs. You, or the group that you are syndicating with, might be desperate for a win after a series of losses or no exits at all. Vet the deal on its own merits, and do it from the beginning.

Is this really an early-stage angel deal? Is the founder still coachable? Will your board members be able to add value and deal with the entrepreneur's new ego? You may also find that you now have the perfect founder; one who understands getting in and getting out on timelines that align with your portfolio strategy and allows you to spend less time mentoring and monitoring. If this is the case, this will allow you to concentrate on deal flow, due diligence for pending deals, and the rest of your portfolio.

For the Entrepreneur

If you have the good fortune to exit on the first attempt, remember lessons you learned about humility and respect. Do not steamroll unsophisticated angels with a new deal that doesn't have the same substance as the first deal. Be careful requesting lenient terms or extraordinarily high valuations because of your track record. It's a different time, and if you've remained in the same industry, the optimal factors that aided you the first time around might have vanished.

Your management team may not have the same level of commitment or loyalty the second time around; they may be planning their own start-up, especially if they cashed out with a lot of money. Don't be lulled by the success you'll enjoy in areas of the country with few growth entrepreneurs. You might find your time diluted by speaking engagements and being asked to serve on boards that may not align with your goals. You need to be fully committed to your next deal if you want to be just as successful.

Takeaway
One simple question: are investors from the CEO's previous deal investing in this deal? If not, you may want to walk away.

52

Work the room: All investors and entrepreneurs need to network

If you aren't good at networking, you will have a difficult time effectively linking-up with other angels and syndicates who will be the key to your success with angel investing. You will also be challenged in driving deal flow without having an army of attorneys, accountants and business networking superstars in your local entrepreneurial community. It's important to overcome this shortfall and learn to be a proficient networker at the various regional, national, and international start-up and early-stage investing events. You will need this skill to seek out independent board members, co-investors, investment bankers and potential exit partners for your portfolio companies. While this can be difficult for you, it needs to be a prerequisite for any entrepreneur you back. They really need to know how to network because, according to you, you won't be able to help. Of course, if you are a solid networker, then you can be more lenient with the entrepreneur.

As a part of your due diligence, make sure to observe the founder in social settings, including introductory meetings with your co-investors. Does he make a point to introduce himself to everyone in the room, or does he stay closely connected to people he brought with him ? How does he follow-up with contacts he has made? Does he understand the power in degrees of separation and creating larger circles of people to work on his behalf? Check the number of contacts he has on sites such as LinkedIn. Create a key metric for the entrepreneur to grow the number of contacts specific to aiding the next phase of his business.

Don't allow a founder to be complacent once he receives funds. If networking is one of your strengths, you might add value as a coach to your founder. Teach him how to effectively network at industry conferences and informally at business functions. Make it a team sport. Perhaps one of the board members knows how to work the room like nobody else. Always huddle after an event to compare names, business cards and sketches on cocktail napkins.

Conversely, many founders are excellent networkers. Networking may be a core competency that's allowed them to bootstrap and develop a working prototype, land beta customers and procure seed stage grants and other funds before they met you. If networking is not your strength, you may find that the founder can help you advance your skill in this area and make you a better angel.

For the Entrepreneur

Networking is a powerful tool for a company designed to exit. It accelerates many aspects of the business, not just sales and marketing. Networking applies to finance and recruiting, to locating better suppliers and complementary technologies that enhance your product offering. Networking can be challenging for scientific founders or technologists who have not dealt directly with customers or had highly public roles in their careers. It may be uncomfortable for you.

If so, you'll need to prove your versatility and willingness to learn and perfect the skill once you're funded. You won't just be networking locally. You'll need to be visible at national conferences or even at international events where you may have to overcome language and cultural barriers. So, start practicing the basics of networking before there is more pressure from your investors.

Takeaway
If you are an introvert (as an investor or an entrepreneur), make sure to add an extrovert to your team.

53

Meet face-to-face; you can learn a lot about the company from body language

Success in angel investing relies heavily on your interpersonal and communication skills. You want your portfolio company founders and management teams to have those same attributes, otherwise you may not enjoy the time spent monitoring the deal. As a result, you might want an exit for the wrong reasons; you might want to do anything to rid yourself of this deal because you no longer trust or enjoy working with the portfolio company.

So how should you monitor a deal? You might think that email and texting is an efficient way to monitor. It is not. Nothing beats having a face-to-face meeting. And that doesn't have to mean at a coffee shop or over breakfast, removed from the action. Meeting the founder on his turf allows you to grasp so much more about the company. As an experienced business person, you will naturally observe events and processes that would otherwise elude you if you base monitoring on electronic communication and remote meeting sites.

The non-personal approach works when things are going well and milestones are being met. But things can get ugly quickly. Face-to-face meetings are critical if there are problems or potential difficulties that threaten your exit timeline or the future of the company. If there's any tension in the deal or with your relationship with the founder, then emails and texts will only become more cryptic and guarded. You may say less than you might otherwise say in person, or you may take on a different tone from the safety of your mobile device.

If you are lucky enough to approach an exit, you'll want to step up in-person visits to ensure clear communication with the entrepreneur. This can be a very stressful time for the founder, and having you close-by gives him the support he needs while keeping you fully informed. As an added bonus, you may have a better chance of discovering if the founder is trying to negotiate a side deal with the acquisition partner if you have a solid and open relationship. You can only blame yourself if you fail to observe what the entrepreneur is doing.

For the Entrepreneur

You should welcome any visit by your investors as an opportunity to teach them more about your business and industry. You want to give them as many chances as possible to interact with all the different facets of your business. Allow them to see you in action with your management team. Let them see your energy and willingness to move things forward to an exit.

You want engaged investors and board members. This is the simple secret. More engagement leads to higher returns for all parties. You want your investors thinking about your business even as they drive away and return home. You want them thinking about you even when they are not there. Remember, angels diversify their investments across several companies. You don't want to be the one they worry about or have to micro-manage. You want to be at the top of their mind for positive attention and for their unique ability to add value. Having a strong working relationship will make future funding rounds, if needed, much easier.

Takeaway

Assign a point person from the syndicate to communicate with the entrepreneur. Don't overwhelm the entrepreneur with multiple visitors each week. Ask the entrepreneur to complete a monthly or quarterly monitoring report, with key metrics, that can be shared with all investors. Include reporting requirements in the term sheet to make sure it gets done.

54

Under full sail: ask the captain for the sales chart

"I understand the product and the market; can you tell me more about sales?" You can halt many a founder in his tracks with that question, especially when you probe beyond the first answer or two. Beyond gross revenue projections, many have simply not considered how it will happen. They blindly believe that the technology or product will be attractive enough to capture a market. In reality, as investors, we know it doesn't happen that way.

Scientific founders and technologists may find it challenging to explain how they will actually sell a product. A founder with a strong corporate marketing background may be incapable of structuring, recruiting and overseeing a small sales organization. With cash at a premium, the company may not be able to justify hiring a seasoned sales executive. This is why you have board members and advisors with deep industry knowledge and contacts involved to help. Since you will most likely need to bootstrap a sales division, it's essential that everyone involved in the business collaborates on this effort.

Founders rarely consider sales operations and fulfillment, since they are so focused on the early-stages of the product and technology. But, it's not just about building a sales team; the founder needs to assemble the right infrastructure to support a sales team. It takes a certain allocation of fixed overhead and there are variable selling expenses to consider, including travel, commissions, referral fees and discounts. Most first-time entrepreneurs will fail to accurately budget for a sales team. A true sales organization is very expensive and well beyond the means of most angel-backed deals. Sometimes a company should just consider outsourcing sales.

Make sure you have an accepted sales plan standard to use in due diligence so you don't get caught underfunding the deal. You'll want to see all possible sales channels identified and ranked. What percentage of the product will be sold through direct sales, sales reps, e-commerce and resellers? Will that mix change over time? How will leads be funneled from marketing and who gets the credit? What is the sales cycle for a new customer? Hopefully, your founder will have been coached to have a sales plan ready. If not, it is a huge cause for concern.

For the Entrepreneur

If sales is not a core competency, find a sales mentor now. If you are seeking early-stage funding, you can't gloss over sales by relying on your product features and the allure of large, profitable markets. Dial up your operational strengths to show you can translate market potential into revenue on a systematic basis. This is a key area where you instill the confidence that you can be Chief Salesman and lead a sales team in the initial phases.

Raising money from friends, family and angels is a kind of sale, but it doesn't help you build business on a larger scale. This is why sales planning and operations are so critical to taking a company to an exit. Acquirers can push a newer product you've developed into existing sales channels, and the revenues generated can be ten times what they were for your small company. Understand the value of selling and make it core to your investor pitch.

Takeaway
Never believe the sales plan. Tear it apart and make the entrepreneur rationalize the thought process. An experienced sales leader on the management team helps. Make sure he is committed and understands what it takes to grow a sales organization with limited cash.

55

Don't pay a lot of money for a hockey stick unless it is signed by Wayne Gretzky

There it is, on the third slide of the founder's presentation deck or buried deep in the business plan. It's the dreaded hockey stick: a sure warning sign that the entrepreneur has been reading a 1998 book about venture capital. To assume absolutely no revenue growth for five years and then project a dramatic uptick in the sixtieth month says something about how much the founder views his product and market. He does not understand why and how people purchase, or the subtle factors and variables that lead to incremental growth. He's more concerned with finding the right template to quickly prove the worth of the company. Reliance on a hockey stick with exaggerated projections is a sign your founder is ultimately not coachable.

Caution: what you want to avoid at all costs is the use of the highly-sophisticated discounted cash flow (DCF) model to value a business, especially an early-stage deal, with hockey stick projections. A DCF is strictly meant to value companies where there is a known history of revenues and profits and a reasonable expectation for sustained, linear growth.

Again, DCF requires a history of sales, not the expectation of sales. Additionally, DCF assumes a fairly stable set of market conditions and constants. It doesn't consider the angel's minority share interest in the company, challenges with liquidity, the size of the deal, or if the company can even develop the technology. Finally, the DCF method is not exit focused. It doesn't consider variables like timing and fluctuation of value due to dilution. If you try to model an early-stage deal, even with discounts, there is no way you are going to be accurate; although you may get lucky if you do enough deals! As an investor, it's best just to avoid the temptation and throw DCF modeling out of your toolbox when conducting due diligence and negotiating the terms of the deal.

Allowing the valuation to be set by a group of experienced angels should lead to more funded deals and a better opportunity for successful exits. If you are investing alone or have only limited experience investing in start-ups, you'll be relying on the inexperienced founder's template formula for valuation. Don't assume it is final or accurate. Everything is negotiable. You want to be able to work closely with a team of investors and the founder to determine a fair value for the company that is based on unique factors and realistic returns, not wishful thinking.

For the Entrepreneur

Angels have become more sophisticated in their valuation methods. They rely on proven tools and best practices that relate specifically to early-stage deals. Don't get trapped daydreaming about the value of your company based on revenue numbers that resemble a hockey stick. It's not real! The discounted cash flow (DCF) method to value a company is typically used by private equity and public financial markets. Remember, those firms are, for the most part, going-concerns with a history of growing or stable revenues and profits; they are not start-ups. It's easy for an entrepreneur to fall into an MBA school's DCF model because it provides a good what-if scenario with unbelievable numbers that benefit the entrepreneur. You'd be amazed at how many entrepreneurs think they are already millionaires on paper even before hiring their first employee. However, what-ifs are not guaranteed and, for the most part, the vast majority of sales projections will not be hit. Not even close. If you insist on using DCF, investors will discount it heavily and most will just walk away from the deal. A pre-money valuation for a start-up should never rely on this valuation methodology. Never.

Definition of Hockey Stick
An unfounded and untested growth assumption represented on a revenue chart as a long flat line that veers upward suddenly at the very end.

Definition of Discounted Cash Flow
Highly-theoretical valuation method projecting a company's ability to generate cash at a future point, then discounting it to determine the present value.

56

The problem is not management, it's the niche idea that looked good but wasn't

While it's true that dominating a niche market is preferable to competing in larger undefined markets, especially for early stage companies, you, the investor, have to be aware of founders who inflate the overall potential of a niche or have misjudged the opportunity altogether. Somehow the allure of going after a niche market captivates entrepreneurs and investors alike. Why wouldn't you go after a market where your resources are more targeted, customers are assumed to be under-served, and revenue should be easily captured?

The trick is not falling into the trap of assuming a niche market actually exists. To verify, you will want the entrepreneur to provide a market feasibility study; it is more complex than market research and goes beyond just conducting focus groups or running A/B tests by email. To truly understand a market niche, you have to possess noteworthy experience and contacts in the specific industry. You'll need to complement your skills of brilliant insight (hunch) and statistical analysis (crunch) with someone who understands how a market niche works, has established connections with people who can help drive adoption, has knowledge of trends, legal and public policy considerations, and has monitored all the start-up and M&A activity within the space.

Many founders you will encounter have some marketing background, but it may not be current experience or they are making more of it than it really was, which of course you will discover during your rigorous reference checks. Maybe your founder took a corporate assignment in marketing, or maybe he gained his marketing experience in another industry. It definitely does not make him an expert. Remember, it is highly possible that you may be especially challenged if you and your co-investors have little understanding of the industry sector. Being unable to identify the positives and negatives of the market can slow due diligence while you hunt for a subject matter expert. You may want to groom a market feasibility expert in your syndication groups, someone who can quickly analyze a niche market, and get the founder to prove the potential value before you invest. If your investment is going to be sizable, consider having an independent study conducted, at the entrepreneur's expense, before moving forward with due diligence. If you can't figure it out, you probably shouldn't invest.

For the Entrepreneur

Some markets are mature, overcrowded and difficult for start-ups to penetrate. You can only compete on scale and low-price. Entrepreneurs have a knack for seeing a niche (literally, a nook) off to the side of the main activity, and building a business around the opportunity.

Be honest as you assess your abilities to analyze and monetize what appears to be a promising niche market. Do you, or someone on your management team, have extensive experience in the overall industry? Understanding a viable niche market comes from thorough primary market research, and personally talking to potential customers, partners and thought leaders. Do you understand the fundamentals and characteristics of the niche? Is it a stable market, or could a quick roll-up of the key players consolidate it quickly? Could a large company like Google change it dramatically in a single weekend with a team of programmers dedicated to creating a new solution?

Takeaway
Make the entrepreneur fund an independent marketing study with a firm that you select. Keep the price low or help negotiate stock options for the marketing firm in exchange for performing the services.

57

Don't expect a company to be great when they never showed you that they can hit par

Driving a golf ball 300 yards with category 1 hurricane winds in your face is tough. Being able to par the hole is even tougher. Entrepreneurs are a lot like professional golfers, except, instead of weather and course conditions, entrepreneurs have a plethora of additional obstacles to deal with. Do you trust, or think, that the entrepreneur you are about to fund has the ability to drive the business from start-up to exit? Well, you better find out.

Start by standardizing your due diligence process and developing a consistent scoring methodology to determine how a company and founder compare to current deal flow, as well as previous deals screened, rejected and funded. Since you don't want to make an emotional decision based on how much you like the product, founder or the market, it's imperative that you are able to categorize and rank the deal according to the founder's track record and potential.

Most likely, you will not have any significant revenue to rely upon. You can, however, look for customers who have agreed to beta test a product. Look at the amount and integrity of primary market research. Does the team assertively go out and talk to decision makers with budgets (corporate), strategic partners and likely consumer purchasers? Or, are the assumptions built on trailing, secondary market research from academic institutions or online sources?

Analyze how the company has deployed seed investment and cash so far. What milestones have been achieved? Assess how much has been diverted away from the critical development path into fixed assets and unnecessary overhead. Have the founders developed any valuable intellectual property? Have they been able to leverage any non-dilutive, non-academic funding like Small Business Innovation Research (SBIR) grants as a temporary funding measure, or are they grant-dependent and unable to adjust to a mindset of quickly growing with revenues?

Make a top level assessment. Use your benchmarks, and compare the company to how your current portfolio companies looked prior to funding. If you're not overly impressed by what you have seen from the founder, take it as a sign and walk away.

For the Entrepreneur

When you're dealing with a group of angels versus an individual investor, expect greater scrutiny on the team you hired responsible for developing the product and market. An investor expects your team to be capable of moving the company to a major inflection point that attracts an acquirer. Have an experienced entrepreneur or investor mentor you on developing and presenting your key milestones in a compelling format. If there are major gaps in research, prototype development or understanding of the market, make sure you address them before you seek funding from investors. Most likely, you will only get one shot to wow an investor. If you fall flat on your face, word will get around that you shopped a deal and got turned down. While most investors won't tell you "no," it will be a long time before you get a second chance to pitch your deal to the same crowd.

Takeaway
It's not about how good an entrepreneur is on the golf course; if an entrepreneur can't drive a company farther than his golf shot, walk away from the deal.

58

Make every entrepreneur tell you their ninety-second elevator pitch

Imagine walking in an elevator on the ground floor of your office building and getting accosted by an entrepreneur looking for funding. You can sit there listening to dribble or you can plainly say, "Give me your elevator pitch. Go!" Getting in and getting out applies to entrepreneurs as much as it applies to you. Founders should be able to quickly articulate the value proposition, and exit potential of their company, in an initial ninety-second pitch, often referred to as an elevator pitch. The objective of the entrepreneur is to get you interested in learning more. Unfortunately, many founders struggle with this simple concept. They want to belabor the highly technical features or discuss the platitudes of "first mover advantage" and "highly innovative" products. You know, as an investor, that those are code-words for needing lots of capital and time to develop a business. Stay away from entrepreneurs who don't understand this. At the same time, beware of the shallow pitch which is succinct and simple because it has no substance. If it sounds like every pitch you heard last week, that echo effect could be telling you to probe deeper. Ask a few questions and see what happens. A pitch that is overly-rehearsed and not solid will crumble with enough inquiry.

You want to get a strong sense of the founder's communication skills. Can he speak clearly and does he make eye contact? Can he move between brevity and in-depth explanation and back again with agility? If an entrepreneur tries to over-talk you during a presentation, is this a sign that he will do the same to potential customers and strategic partners? A speech is a kind of proxy for cash. If you ask for a ninety-second elevator pitch and the founder rambles on for three minutes, what implication does that have for the money you are about to invest? Can he follow basic instructions? Is he coachable? If the entrepreneur can't finish a pitch in ninety seconds, will he run over on the time it takes to get to an exit?

If, after all this, you are still interested in the deal, invite the entrepreneur to give you a full presentation. Are you relieved that the elevator ride is over?

For the Entrepreneur

Think third grade. Keep it simple and make the investor want to ask you questions. Admittedly, your elevator pitch is potentially delivered to highly-educated and successful professionals, but that doesn't mean they have the time or interest to hear you drone on about your innovative, first-mover advantage, absolutely-guaranteed product or service. You need a clear, concise and compelling bite-sized executive summary ready to ship. Make it simple to say and make it contagious, you want investors talking about the deal when you aren't in the room.

The movie industry has mastered the elevator pitch and has it down to a single sentence: "(insert blockbuster movie) meets (insert other blockbuster movie)." Your audience is either hooked or they're not. Even with a highly-technical or scientific innovation, the brevity and gravity of the elevator pitch will resonate with the people who can really help you with funding: business people. Downplay features and dial-up benefits. Position the major pain points and the addressable market. Going up?

> **Definition of Elevator Pitch**
> A ninety-second summary used to quickly and simply define a product or service and its value proposition, literally in the amount of time it would take to deliver on an elevator ride. Perfected by few and bungled by many.

59

If you find a fatal flaw in a deal, kill it early. Entrepreneurs are counting on a positive response: "Obi Wan, you are my only hope"

Many entrepreneurs get to a point in the funding cycle where they are desperate. They are teetering on the edge of closing up shop if they can't get capital. To make it worse, you may be the last shot at continuing their dream. As an individual investor, you can't let those emotions impact your decision. If you are going to pass, let it be known quickly so other options can be considered . You want to be fair; you should not be conducting due diligence on more than three deals at any one time. As you know, it takes a lot of personal time to analyze an industry, to perform feasibility studies of a new product, and to determine the amount of capital required to market at scale. The checklist of due diligence materials can be endless. Do you really believe that you have the time to devote to another deal?

When you are thinking about the valuation, the term sheet, which board members are best suited for the particular deal, and how the company fits into your portfolio distribution strategy, it can be a full-time job. It takes a lot of time and effort to do each one right. If you have a huge syndication group, you can spread out the due diligence workload.

If you find a fatal flaw in due diligence, kill the deal right away and give your attention to the deals with promise. A "fatal flaw" is not a problem that you wish wasn't there or merely an inconvenience, but rather something that no matter how you approach the problem, would be a complete bar to your getting the deal done. The entrepreneur is counting on you for a positive response, so you are helping him by removing any false hope of funding. You are not responsible for the fate of the company. Entrepreneurs are easily frustrated because they have a lot on the line professionally and personally. You don't have to be too polite or considerate at this point. Don't waste the entrepreneur's time if you're not ready to commit, especially if you don't have the time to lead an investment.

You can inform the entrepreneur that now is not the right time for funding by you or your syndication. You can keep the door open. If you explain that the deal is just not right for you and you ask the founder to keep you posted, you still have the opportunity to get back in the game as the round fills out.

For the Entrepreneur

If you're not going to be funded, you want to know right away so you can consider other options. You don't want to back an angel into a corner and tell him he is the only hope to keep the company alive. Angel investors don't like to be given ultimatums; it's a complete turnoff and your desperation will spread quickly.

Be patient during due diligence, but also be prepared to provide information quickly. Some investors will go line by line through your business plan, while others may ignore it completely and make their own assumptions. Others will look at the representations you made in the formal presentation and compare that to the documents you've submitted for due diligence. Do the financials make sense? Is everything the founder said true? Is there enough here that I like and trust in order to jump in?

> **Takeaway**
> Never work on more than three deals at one time. It takes a lot of time and effort to do a deal right. Spreading your efforts will dilute the quality of your work.

60

Standardize your due diligence report

For the past few years, organizations like the Angel Capital Association and the Angel Resource Institute have promoted angel investing and sharing of best practices across the United States and around the globe. As a result, many angel funds and groups have formally adopted these suggestions as a way to improve returns. The good news is that there are enough resources out there that you won't have to invent much of anything. The trick is finding what works for you and following it religiously. Don't get stuck doing a deal that you make exceptions for; chances are it will fail.

One of the most useful practices when deciding on an investment opportunity is using a standardized due diligence process and checklist (visit 100rules.com for a sample checklist.) While most items are mandatory, there will be situations where the stage of the business may be very early and some information will not be available. Regardless of this, make sure to create standard forms for reference checks, market and product analysis, and site visits. Once complete, develop a standard due diligence summary report that covers every possible area of discovery (there can be hundreds). You'll want a way to rank the major sections. Create a scoring model that can be used to compare prospective deals against other companies you have taken through due diligence. Since every deal falls short in several areas, you might have a mechanism to document where you believe risks can be mitigated with more information or with short-term corrections by the founders. The report should help you conduct advance work for negotiating and closing a deal.

While there are some experienced angels who will advise you to keep early-stage deal documentation to a minimum, you need to decide what level of documentation is enough to make you comfortable with making an investment. By formalizing due diligence, and what is expected from entrepreneurs from the beginning, you should be able to shorten the time period required to make a decision and, given this, your deal flow should increase along with your ability to manage multiple investments across your portfolio.

For the Entrepreneur

It can be difficult, in the middle of a full sprint, to pause and direct your full attention on the intricacies of landing an angel investment. As a first-time entrepreneur, there are many concepts and legal matters to learn quickly. Make sure you have mentors along the way, especially a serial entrepreneur who will give you informal but candid guidance. Someone with an exit will be the most valuable, because he will understand the benefits of the angel model.

You should also expect guidance and consistency from the angels you approach. Make sure the angel or angel group clearly spells out expectations, timelines and instructions for every phase, including initial screening, due diligence, negotiations and closing the round. They do appreciate it when you adhere to the process they communicate. It's the first sign you're coachable!

> **Takeaway**
> Entrepreneurs should ask the investor for a due diligence checklist early in the process so they can get a start on assembling the necessary documents.

61

Understand what you are buying; sometimes less is more

Too many investors get hung up on how many shares of a company they own versus the percentage of equity. Watch for entrepreneurs and sophisticated attorneys who take full advantage of this when they create the original capitalization table.

If you ever talk to an entrepreneur who says he will sell you a million shares of the company for $100,000, you know he is trying to mask the true value. Many unsophisticated investors will think, "Wow, I just got something worth $1 million for only $100,000." Honestly, you don't have a clue how many other shares are outstanding or what percentage of the business you are buying. You would rather have the entrepreneur tell you that your $100,000 investment will get X% of the business; this method puts an actual value on the deal.

You can fool anyone (initially) if you create a way of masking value. For example, would you rather own one share of Berkshire Hathaway A Shares (BRK-A) or a thousand shares of Microsoft (MSFT)? Why would you only want to own one share of any stock? You'd rather own a thousand shares of Microsoft, right? But that's not the right answer. In 2012, one share of Berkshire was worth over $130,000 while a thousand shares of Microsoft was worth only $28,000. As an investor, you need to ask what percentage of the company an investment will yield? How many shares are authorized and outstanding? What was the price per share of the most recent round? Is there an employee, board, or key management stock option pool?

Use caution when dealing with entrepreneurs who try to avoid the valuation questions by allowing their attorney's to create a Private Placement Memorandum ("PPM"). If an entrepreneur provides you with a PPM, it does not mean you can't change the rules. In fact, if the entrepreneur thinks that he is going to dictate the terms with a PPM, he's probably not coachable. He also just wasted $5,000 - $25,000 on attorney fees to write a document that won't be used. Throw the PPM and the deal out the door.

For the Entrepreneur

Private investors are becoming more and more sophisticated. As they make more investments and diversify their portfolios, they are learning quickly how to mitigate risk. As investors syndicate with other investment groups, they gain the advantage of many more resources for due diligence and company valuation.

It's better to work with investors on how they want to value the company to gauge their level of interest in an investment. Any special formula that you devise to inflate the value of the company, or in any way make it difficult to clearly determine value, will only hurt your credibility. It could either delay getting to funding, or cause you to be removed from consideration immediately.

Takeaway
Do not let the entrepreneur dictate the terms or mask value with financial tricks. Vet every deal using the same due diligence tools so that you can make a fair assessment of your investments and potential returns.

62

Being a first mover does not have all the advantages they teach in business school

An entrepreneur who wants you to fund him based on the company's first mover advantage could represent the very first deal to fail in your portfolio. A first mover advantage is very expensive. It's easy to get trampled in an untapped market by the other companies arriving right behind you; even worse, they learned from your mistakes and are drafting off your marketing efforts. So, do you really want to fund a first mover? The answer is, it depends.

The fact is you have to invest significantly in marketing for a first mover product to be successful. You're potentially in a worse position than a second or third mover who can wait long enough for the market to become more defined and mature before releasing a competing product or service.

You will find that inexperienced entrepreneurs haven't taken the time to analyze the future value of a business in a mature market. In their minds, it's easier to raise funds around the allure of a new market. However, most entrepreneurs are not sophisticated enough to understand that the cost to educate a new market generally exceeds the cost to compete in an existing market. They may not fully understand the new market, either. They won't know how large and complex the market is, or how dispersed and fragmented it might become.

As a result, will you really be able to get all the way to an exit if you back a first mover advantage strategy, or will your cash be consumed from building out infrastructure for somebody else to leverage? Do you want to be the first home in a new neighborhood that has to pay for the road, electric lines, sewer and other resources that the other houses will get to take advantage of? The answer is "only if you can charge them for doing so." If you decide to move forward, you should certainly allocate a higher ratio of dry powder for the investment. You will need many more rounds of investment to support the unknown costs of marketing and a longer time period for the product to get widely adopted.

Some entrepreneurs are exceptional at identifying new markets and others are better at building companies. Let another company design, build and establish the market before you enter. If you're confident your company has the resources to be the first mover, raise enough money to be the second mover also.

For the Entrepreneur

Don't ruin your credibility with investors by claiming that you don't have competitors or that you hold a first mover advantage in a new market. Even if you're right, it demonstrates you don't understand how expensive it is to educate a market. It also begs the obvious question, why isn't anyone else in there right now if it's so lucrative? It's like the penguins that huddle closely on an ice floe; nobody wants to be on the outer edge or first in the water for a reason.

First mover advantage is no longer a compelling lever for raising funds. Your angels are interested in a profitable exit. They don't want to become entrenched with the effort and expense to build out a market. For example, in difficult economic times, corporate buyers tend not to switch suppliers. A buyer won't be fired for sticking with a proven vendor, but he could be fired for trying a new one that fails.

Takeaway
You have to invest significantly in marketing for a product to be successful. If you have enough money to have first mover advantage, make sure you have enough funds to win second place as well.

63

Lost in translation: Some research projects should remain benched

Walk the hall of any research university around the country and this will happen to you: You will see a deal that makes you stop in your tracks. The company has summarized the key benefits clearly and demonstrates a fast-track pathway to commercialization. What you see captivates you and does not let you think about much else. It may be compelling on its own merits, or it may solve a problem in an area that you know well.

There are billions of dollars pouring into university research labs and under the mandates of federal technology transfer laws, you may have the opportunity to see some amazing science that has the ambition to leave the lab and monetize itself in the marketplace. We wouldn't have most of our aviation, automotive, internet or telecommunications technology without inventions originally designed and funded for defense purposes. Yet that doesn't mean you should pick up just any idea that federal funding started; most will never materialize into anything.

While you may be tempted to suspend reality and pass the deal along to due diligence, you can do your fellow investors a favor by applying more scrutiny when gating and screening deals. Ask more questions. Seek out companies that are in the field for guidance, rather than other scientists. Many early-stage research companies are wily enough to live on "fumes" for several years, cobbling together enough grants to keep the thing alive, yet not necessarily commercially viable.

Most scientific founders are not proficient in conducting primary market research, instead counting on huge markets with secondary (and trailing) market data. They have a tendency to avoid pressing the research to the point of failure, hoping that early-stage investors will not know enough to scrutinize the critical milestones of a technical product. Most importantly from an angel's perspective, what does a realistic exit look like for a research company, and what milestones will need to be reached to engage a potential buyer? Knowing the right questions to ask can save you from making a bad investment.

For the Entrepreneur

You may be a recognized and formidable scientist, inventor and innovator. After years of painstaking research, and trial and error, you and your team truly have invented a breakthrough product or service. It stands apart. It has been validated with grant funding for prototype and proof of concept in the technology field, or pre-clinical work in the medical field. But do angels or potential buyers care?

It will help you to understand that while angels consider funding early-stage companies, there are many times when a technology is either too far ahead of its time or not refined enough for commercial applications and revenue generation. This can be a matter of degree, and obvious gaps to commercialization may not come to light until you have gone too far into due diligence. An exit has to be within sight; otherwise, it will be extremely difficult to get funded.

Takeaway
Significant government investment may signal the next great industry, but don't get trapped. Millions will pour into these early stage deals on a hope and a prayer. With the ever-present Internet and flow of information, investors need to recognize that research is not limited to a single university, state or country. If we are working on a new technology here, others are also working on it elsewhere in the world.

64

Know the difference between a great showman and an entrepreneur who is a great leader

Ask an experienced start-up investor about the qualities that make up good leadership, especially for early-stage deals, and you may be surprised by how you are answered. For the most part, don't expect to hear about having solid communication skills, an ability to rally a team, a vision for the future and an aptitude to follow a roadmap. No, what you will probably hear about is that most of the entrepreneurs, in the investor's portfolio of companies, should be replaced because they are not the leaders they thought they were when they wrote the investment check. Many entrepreneurs may have presented well in the beginning and were great salespeople, but they do not have the characteristics required to take the company all the way to an exit. Even worse, they don't know how to listen.

There will be early signs showing you when you do not have a great leader at the helm of a deal. There may be multiple rounds of funding in the company; suggesting they did not plan well or their ability to operate was ineffective. Or maybe not even a single investor, from any prior round, is reinvesting in the new round. Why is that? Leaders should inspire loyalty and be capable of building great teams through interpersonal skills.

Other warning signs may include a leader who manages by issuing ultimatums. You might spot this at a first introduction when the founder tells you he has a hard deadline, that he has to have the money within two weeks or else. That's a big turnoff. How about the tactic of telling you he has another deal on the table to see if you'll bid more? Do you really want to back that type of leader?

A common mistake of investors is to misconstrue passion for ability. You might have a good feeling from a positive first meeting, but that may be artificial. Never make an investment based on one meeting. Hold multiple meetings to see if the founder's level of passion is consistent, or to see if the stress level changes during certain topics. Introduce different levels of stress in a meeting. Mix up the questions and the roles of each angel from meeting to meeting to see how a founder reacts. If the

142

answers aren't consistent, walk away. Unfortunately, if you already have a portfolio company with a poor leader, try to step in and coach them on the skills required to be successful. You'll know at that point if the deal is worth saving.

For the Entrepreneur

Make an assessment of your leadership ability now. Are you really the right person to lead the company? An angel might not agree. You may be the person with the big ideas, or you are the most comfortable out on stage and selling the product all day long. That won't be enough. Investors are not looking for figureheads. They want to back somebody who knows all aspects of the company, who knows about finances, costs and running a business.

You don't want to be the one with the exceptional sales talent who doesn't know the numbers. You don't want to be the one who pauses during a presentation with a question about finances and calls up the chief financial officer for the answer. You will need to be able to speak to every part of the business, especially the finances. Investors want to know where their cash is being allocated.

> **Takeaway**
> Great showmanship does not make an entrepreneur a great leader. You need a good leader to make a deal successful.

65

Take advantage of investment tax credits; it lowers risk, but don't overpay

As many people know, and others choose to ignore, small businesses drive local economies and employment. That's why many state governments now offer tax credits to high net worth investors. The states want to spur investments in early-stage companies by incenting investors to fund deals that are not fundable by banks. In fact, over half of all states offer tax credits or are considering them. It's a highly-charged political issue related to job creation and tax-breaks for wealthy individuals. The sad part is that these are not really tax-breaks; they are tax credits for the dollars invested in local businesses that are, for the most part, pre-approved by each state. Investors are actually risking a lot of their personal wealth to stimulate the local economies. While the tax credits are really not that important at this stage of the game, they do allow a way for investors to lower the up-front risk for each deal.

If you use North Carolina as an example, the Securities Division of the Department of the Secretary of State administers the Qualified Business Tax Credit Program and certifies certain "qualified businesses" as defined by state statutes. An investor may receive up to 25% of the amount invested as a credit against future state tax liability. In 2013, the business had to be actively engaged in manufacturing, processing, research and development, or a service-related industry with revenue not exceeding $5,000,000 (five million dollars.) The state has a maximum tax credit per year allowed by individuals and collectively as a group. Under this program, if an individual investor makes a $50,000 investment in a qualified business, the individual will receive a tax credit of $12,500 to use the following calendar year. This effectively guarantees that the investor will see a minimum of 25% back on his investment, even if the company fails. Other states have similar programs.

However, despite the intention of the state, some entrepreneurs take advantage of these tax credits and try to artificially inflate the pre-money valuations. But no tax credit comes close to covering up the risks of a bad deal. As an investor, you need to forget about the tax credits and base your negotiations with entrepreneurs on the deal itself. Don't overpay for the company. The tax credit lowers risk of a complete loss, but it is not guaranteed in some states and should never be the basis for making an investment.

Buyer Beware: There are some companies that stay alive indefinitely, that should have been killed off years ago. They have a knack not for getting to an exit, but of continually finding new investors (uneducated or those new to investing in early-stage deals) who believe the risk drops with something like an investment tax credit. Don't be one of those investors.

For the Entrepreneur

Align your interests with investors. There are many tools and tricks out there that seek to manipulate key concepts associated with valuation, term sheets and board structure. Sophisticated, experienced angels do not fall for most of these tools. They've seen them before, they're not persuasive, and mostly they will reduce your credibility with potential investors.

You want to show that you're coachable, a great leader and the best choice for leading the company forward. You want to demonstrate that you are an excellent communicator and salesperson, but you also have the numbers down cold. The financial reports you'll provide to your board will be impeccable and timely. You will be anticipating risk and asking for help from your board before they see the problem.

You're not going to allow the start-up to languish as a lifestyle business. This thought process is more valuable than any tax credit. Investors need multiples on their money, not pennies on the dollar.

Takeaway
No tax credits come close to covering up the risk of a bad deal.

66

Does everyone have a new car and nice office furniture? Don't pay for it

You might notice something peculiar when you visit the company: a credenza and bookcase from Ethan Allen in the founder's office, a high-end coffee maker in the break room or several new electric cars outside. If they're not flying coach, prepare to coach.

It's not really about the furniture. It's about losing the laser-focus to reach an exit. It's not just the money but the time lost being off-task. You don't want your founder purchasing tangible fixed assets and comfort, when what he really needs to be acquiring with your money is intelligence. You want him re-investing the angel funds in value-added intangibles: product and pricing knowledge, sales and marketing intelligence, distribution know-how, competitor intelligence, customer lists and preferences. There typically is not a positive multiple that an acquirer will pay for a Herman Miller chair, so why decrease the value of invested dollars so quickly?

If you have a scientific founder, be careful that he is not investing the money in sophisticated lab and diagnostic equipment. Check for artificial layers of management hierarchy on the organization chart. Remind him that he is no longer operating on a federal grant-funding business model. Have a board member mentor him in the use of general business services, contract research organizations and contract manufacturing.

It might be miscellaneous business expenses like travel. There are fine lines that dictate the stewardship of funds. While you're certainly not happy paying for someone to fly first class, it may actually be worth the $200 seat upgrade so the entrepreneur can have room to work productively on the five-hour return flight. That's good judgment. Have him review his travel schedule when he's attending a conference. Will he see prospects and potential suppliers while he's in town?

Set expectations early. Always ask for a Use of Funds plan. Share your purchasing philosophy with the founder. You don't want to have to go out and raise money again, or resort to venture capital funding, because the cash was spent on something other than an exit trajectory.

INVESTOR PERSPECTIVE

For the Entrepreneur

Getting to the exit takes an incredible amount of focus. Your investors understand this and have expectations of how your time and their cash should be spent. Be frugal with fixed asset purchases and overhead expenses. Stewardship and transparency is critical when working with hands-on angels. Align your expectations early.

While you need to have some comforts to be productive, selecting nice office furniture is the kind of distraction you don't need. Be prudent with travel expenses and be as efficient as possible on a business trip. Divide and conquer across several industry conferences. You and your team may now be enjoying steady salaries, possibly more money than you might have been earning as you bootstrapped the business. Now is not the time to splurge on personal luxuries.

Just as your board is there to mentor you, you need to set an example for management team members.

Takeaway
Ask the entrepreneur for a Use of Funds during the vetting process and hold them to it.

RULES TO HELP INVESTORS & ENTREPRENEURS WORK TOGETHER TO BUILD A BETTER COMPANY

ENTREPRENEUR PERSPECTIVE

67

The investor writing the biggest check shouldn't automatically get a board seat

A standard term sheet for a seed or series A round of investment generally requires a three or five person board of directors. A three person board is comprised of the founder, a representative for the lead investor group and an "independent" board member who will bring industry expertise. A five person board is similar; however, the founder will elect two representatives, the investors will elect two representatives, and there will be one independent member.

Putting the board together is easier said than done. Many new and disorganized groups of investors tend to let the person writing the largest check become their representative on the board. In most angel deals, the syndicate will have a dominant investor who puts in more money than anyone else. As a result, the biggest investor's expectations often match the size of their checks. They think that money means a seat on the board of the company or the ability to dictate terms beyond what is reasonable to the other investors. This can be dangerous. In fact, having them on the board could be a liability.

While the investor with the deepest pockets may have the financial means, it does not mean that he has the skill set to work with an entrepreneur or to guide an early-stage company. The largest investor in the deal may come from the corporate world and may not understand the specific industry of the company or the intricacies of exit-focused angel investing. He could be looking for the home run versus a solid double or triple. It's not to say that you don't want your lead investor involved, you do; but, is the investor the right person to dictate the terms of the deal and capable of being an active board member? It's tough, from your perspective, when 90% of the funding is coming from one person; the tendency of all investors, and the entrepreneur, will be to defer to their demands. Try to set expectations up front. If the lead investor wants to dictate terms, serve on the board, and be the liaison for the syndicate, but if your gut tells you this is not going to work, it's okay to walk away before writing the first check. Remember, you want to invest in companies that have strong boards, strong management, and a great concept. If the stars aren't aligned, get out before you get in.

For the Entrepreneur

If you're funded by an angel group, you'll see only one check from that group in each round even though several or all of the angels in the group have funded the deal. Because of this, you may not see that one individual may have put in a disproportionately high amount compared to everyone else. The group doesn't want you, as the founder, appeasing one investor, when what is most important to an exit is the team of investors. You should insist that a board member have domain expertise and "bring something more" than a large wallet to the table.

This is the strength of the designed-for-acquisition angel model. The focus is not on who put the most money into the deal. The emphasis is on putting the right people in place to make the company a success. That primarily happens during due diligence when the angels identify a subject-matter expert from your industry who can help them understand the deal and potentially serve as the independent board member to drive the company toward a quick exit.

Takeaway
Make sure your group understands the dynamics between the largest check writer and the company's need for sound board leadership. You want a board member who has domain expertise representing your investment. If that person writes the largest check, great; otherwise, pick expertise over the size of their wallet.

68

Always have a balanced board

As a start-up and early-stage investor, you will need to think a lot about board structure and make up. Boards are critical to the overall success of the business from the first day of operation to the day the company exits. It's important to think of the board as the pistons in an engine. Without the pistons, the car's not going anywhere and who would want to buy it? In terms of angel deals, most companies will utilize a five person board: two board members appointed by the majority of investors, two board members appointed by the founders, and an independent board member mutually agreed to by the other board members. You won't see too much deviation from this structure, at least for the first two rounds of investment. Conceptually, the number of board members and the non-biased resources of the independent board member creates a foundation for successful and more effective communication and management. There is a reason the investor-to-founder board ratio works; it takes into account the important role that your cash and experience have in relation to the promise of an entrepreneur's idea.

Remember, a strong and engaged board, with industry knowledge and connections, will lead to a stronger exit. When the board sets expectations early in the relationship, the entrepreneur will understand the direction and prioritize accordingly. Each will know clearly which behaviors are and are not appropriate. As additional monitoring, the board will deploy basic governance tools such as quarterly financial reports and monthly updates to all investors supplemented with specific management metrics related to milestones and key inflection points that are believed to be critical to the success of the business. Don't discount the value of consistency and setting of the tone early on. The board and the entrepreneur will appreciate knowing what to expect. Make sure, especially in the early development of the company, that the board meets regularly, on a formal basis and in person every month. It may be challenging if board members live a great distance away; however, if a board member can't make meetings, is he really engaged? If you aren't serving on the board, request observer rights in the board room so you can monitor, first-hand, the progress of the business.

Boards function to assist with, not to control the direction of the company. Early-stage boards should be working boards, not reporting boards. They should be hands-on, engaging sessions where investors and management drive the company toward an exit. You don't want "yes men" sitting in the board seats. As an angel, you may dictate board requirements in the deal terms; however, you must be prepared to act accordingly if the entrepreneur, or current board, fails to follow through or becomes lackadaisical. Investors elect board members and may replace them if necessary.

For the Entrepreneur

The board helps you set the direction of the company and helps navigate change when inevitably something will require a modification in the plan or timeline. Keep your board well informed. They are the conduits to your investors and, together with good reporting standards, will make it much easier to raise your next round of money.

Board size and structure is usually non-negotiable, especially for a new entrepreneur who has never taken a company to exit and is putting little cash in the deal. The standard board arrangement is designed to get your company to an exit. The strict consistency works in your favor. It means the board is mitigating the risk of failure on your behalf and bringing in even more resources to help you.

Early-stage boards are made up of highly knowledgeable and well-connected individuals both in and out of your industry. They are based on a growing body of best practices uniquely structured for angel investing. Your board is specialized in nature and will have little in common with large corporate boards or venture-capital backed companies. If you find yourself funded by an angel or group that is relaxed with its approach to boards, your chance of a successful exit is limited. A strong and active board will help you build a stronger company.

> **Takeaway**
> If there are three or more founders, decide which ones are okay with not holding a board seat; otherwise, it can get messy. This can be a reason not to invest.

69

Create a compensation committee

Every founder and start-up junkie hates this one, but it is something that every deal needs. Once a board is created, one of the first duties is to form a compensation committee. The committee will typically have two members, usually the independent board member and one of the board members representing the investors. Note that the founder, if active in the daily management of the company, should never participate in the compensation committee; there exists too much conflict of interest.

The compensation committee oversees the yearly salary and bonus amounts for the CEO, the senior management team, and even the board itself. It sets the year-over-year strategy for salary and stock options, if applicable. While this committee will most likely need a majority of the board members to approve any recommendations, depending on the investment terms, it's important to remember that company representatives, as well as the founders, will have some say in the matter. Serving on this committee is a big responsibility and can be highly emotionally charged, especially if the company is running low on fumes.

As an investor and board member, you want an entrepreneur to take home just enough money to pay his monthly overhead expense, but not too much money that may adversely impact the burn rate of the invested cash on-hand. If you pay too little, the company may risk losing key members of the management team that are needed to drive the company toward an exit. Your aim is to protect shareholders, which sometimes does involve protecting the management team.

If the board or investors and entrepreneur hit an impasse over compensation, think about finding someone with human resources experience to coach an inexperienced compensation committee. You want someone who understands how to quickly build comparative and dynamic salary and compensation information for the industry and the stage of the company that may be used to make an informed and less emotional decision. If available, you can determine compensation ranges from within your own portfolio, from other angel groups or from a national database service. In reality, sometimes it just comes down to what the company can afford.

As you get more experience in this area, you are not only building a compensation infrastructure for one particular portfolio company, you are creating a template you can use across all of your companies (And setting expectations for future management teams.) It can be a huge distraction to the performance and day-to-day management of your portfolio company if not managed appropriately. Don't ignore compensation. Learn to manage it.

For the Entrepreneur

Like the pre-money valuation and the content of the term sheet, what the board compensation committee decides for salaries and incentives may not match your expectations. Do you really want to fight to the death over salary and benefits? Is that why you founded the company?

You may need to reassess your position on this issue and coach other people on your team who feel they're not being fairly compensated. You'll need to rely on the larger opportunity and the longer-term payoff of an exit.

If you do have justification that someone's compensation is way below market rate, make a rational case for the recommendation and abide by the compensation committee's decision. Do not try to create alternative or creative forms of compensation that, once revealed, will destroy your integrity with investors. Accept that the compensation committee is in a tight spot and you are in a tight spot.

Takeaway
In most cases, investors will rarely see an early-stage investment where the founders are paid too little; most deals way overpay the entrepreneur. An overpaid entrepreneur isn't incentivized to sell the company. Look at standard compensation surveys in the industry to calibrate salary expectations, then reduce by 30% or more for the first few years and offer the entrepreneur goals to reach a bonus. Keep the entrepreneur hungry or this could turn into a lifestyle business.

70

Create an audit committee (not including the founder)

Fact: a strong board, and even stronger board monitoring, will lead to stronger exits sooner. It's not difficult to see how this works. The more an investor is educated about all aspects of the company's operational and financial performance, the more likely he is to stay active with the company and want to participate in a follow-on financing round. While information itself is good, investors want to make sure the information they are getting is also accurate and actionable.

In addition to compensation committees, which were discussed in Rule 10, most boards should also create an audit committee. While the primary goal of this committee is to audit the company's financial statements, a secondary goal is to manage the company's risk profile. Risk is not just tied to the financial statements. Is the company operating in an ethical manner? Is the company following all required and mandated regulations for the industry? The list of questions can go on for pages. The point is that the audit committee protects the company and the board against actions of an employee that could derail the business. Think about a rogue employee who bribes a public official for a major contract or an entrepreneur who ships out product to a fictitious customer in order to book revenue this quarter at the expense of the next quarter. This happens every day and the impact on the business is devastating. An audit committee is usually made up of two to three board members, with one member, at a minimum, having a solid understanding of financial statements, taxation, and operations management. The committee keeps reports up-to-date and ready for future investors, or more importantly for potential exit partners to review. You never know when the opportunity to sell the business is going to present itself, so be prepared.

One of the main tasks for the audit committee is to review monthly and quarterly financial statements before they are forwarded to investors. While most fiscal year-end financial statements are prepared in-house, or by a company's independent accountant to keep the cost involved low, there are some incidents where a full audit, conducted by a CPA firm, is required. Full audits can be extremely expensive, especially for a start-up. It can be in the range of $5,000 to $15,000 or more, depending on complexity and location. If the company takes on bank debt, it is likely that the bank will require audited statements. As an investor, you should feel good about a board that understands the role of an audit committee. Make sure this is not a rubber-stamping committee and that the players understand how mitigating risk can help a company position itself for success.

For the Entrepreneur

If you don't have a strong financial background, when it comes to preparing, distributing and understanding financial reports, make sure you have a mentor who can help you communicate and cooperate with the board's audit committee. This could be one of the most critical areas when working with a board and it can be challenging because it appears to take your attention away from the product, customers and your management team.

While you may not have a strong financial background, you are now at an advanced stage where it will help to become more educated about the income statement, balance sheet and cash flow statement. Even if it is not required in the term sheet, take the time to prepare a brief financial summary for the audit committee, hitting the high notes from the previous quarter. Research variances ahead of time and have potential remedies underway. Consider every financial decision through the perspective of the audit committee and your investors.

Takeaway
Companies can spend hundreds of thousands of dollars restating earnings upon an exit and may even then lose the exit or next round of financing if they don't have good accounting practices. An audit committee should work with solid CPA firms to make sure the company's financial statements are in correct GAAP format and accurate. Don't ask Uncle Phil to do your taxes.

71

Keep your powder dry

Musket-firing soldiers in the Revolutionary War stored and carried their gunpowder in separate containers, like powder horns, in order to maintain the integrity of their weapons so they could live to fight another day. They always wanted to have enough "dry powder" on hand to fire.

As an early-stage investor, you'll spend a good deal of time strategizing and anticipating events, like exits, which will happen far in the future. While that can be a fun part of the process, there will be times the events actually require additional funding capital. For an early-stage company, it is nearly impossible to forecast cash needs a year or two out. "Stuff happens" as the phrase goes, and something almost always goes wrong that delays the cash flow. As a result, from our experience, ninety (90%) percent of early-stage companies need more cash than projected, and you and the current investors in the portfolio company will most likely be the only viable means to fund the shortfall. This is where "dry powder" comes into play. Dry powder is the amount of capital reserved on the sidelines that an investor allocates for future investments in the same portfolio company. For the most part, investors allocate this capital because they recognize that most start-ups and early-stage companies will need multiple rounds of funding. If you, as an investor, don't invest in future rounds, your ownership percentage in the company will be severely diluted. Know the implications.

Dry powder is usually allocated at a ratio of 1 to 1 or up to 3 to 1, depending on investor preference and the method by which an investor invests. Having one to three times the original investment in reserve (mentally or physically in a fund) for each deal allows the investor to continue to support the portfolio company in future rounds. Experienced investors have learned that if they want to be in the company for the long-haul and to protect their equity share, then they need to have additional capital ready to deploy into each deal for the second and third rounds. It almost always takes more money and more time to reach an exit than agreed to in the original projections.

Beware of excessive reliance on dry powder: It's like duct tape and will only keep a sinking ship afloat for so long. Don't let those large capital reserves lure you into lax board monitoring or from keeping pressure on the founder to perform. It should also be noted that there are some very successful funds and Angels who only make one investment in a deal and choose not to reserve dry powder. Learn what works best for you, given your risk profile.

For the Entrepreneur

Getting to an exit takes two to three times as long as you think it will take. You and your team will attempt to create the realistic projections for how long it takes to develop your products, penetrate the markets and scale to an exit. The job of the angel investor is to have reserves ready to help when things don't go as planned.

Don't be offended with investors who are taking issue with your projections; they are setting aside dry powder to avoid unforeseen circumstances and future dilution.

Definition of Dry Powder
Reserved and/or committed capital that creates a financial cushion in case the deal needs more funding than expected. Dry powder is formally allocated by angel investors in recognition of the longer time periods and unanticipated expenses required to make an early-stage company attractive to an acquirer and exit successfully. In most cases, the investor has the right not to make a follow-on investment.

Protect your investment with tough, yet fair, terms

You're keenly aware of the odds of backing a rookie entrepreneur with an unproven technology and markets that are not fully defined. Statistically, there's a better than even chance you won't see an exit or get your money back. As an angel, you mitigate that risk by conducting a thorough due diligence with other investors, putting in place a strong board of directors for governance, finding an independent board member with related industry knowledge, while keeping the company focused through consistent monitoring and detailed milestones.

In addition, you did a terrific job protecting both the investors and the founders against dilution from venture capital funding; you and your syndication partners allocated more than enough dry powder around the table to take the company through multiple rounds of funding, if needed. You and the founder are in this fight together. You know that you both could suffer a cram-down on your ownership percentage, or even a complete failure, if you're not working cooperatively to push the company forward.

Despite this seemingly great relationship, you didn't agree to easy terms to appease a brilliant or charismatic founder. You didn't want to loosen your standards because your deal flow may have been light, or because you really wanted to make one more investment before the year was done to diversify your portfolio. During due diligence and negotiations, you looked closely at the return potential and the future funding needs. You ran dilution scenarios ahead of time and recognized the need for like-minded investors with an ability to reserve enough dry powder to keep the lights on. You explained to the entrepreneur and your co-investors why the terms needed to be so restrictive. In fact, with all the work you did, the founder was on the same page with you and understood that the risk you were taking was as high as his risk running a company with a small salary.

While your entrepreneur quickly agreed to the terms, most don't. If you get too much push back from an entrepreneur, you may want to reconsider making an investment because negotiations at the time of the exit will be even harder to discuss. No matter how much you like the entrepreneur, insist on anti-dilution provisions, liquidation preferences, voting rights, and protective provisions in the term sheet. If you don't understand what each means, learn it so you don't get caught in a compromising position. Make sure you maximize your percentage ownership in every round of investment and do your best to protect your partners' interests as well, that includes your co-investors and the management team. This is a team sport.

For the Entrepreneur

You're in this together, you and the angel. There might be tension as you learn to work together and you may initially bristle under having a board of directors monitoring the company. That's good discipline against even greater risk. What you're really trying to do is avoid a venture capitalist from coming in and diluting everyone's equity stake. If you cannot get to an exit on the angel rounds alone and a venture capitalist funds the next round, you will most likely be replaced as the chief executive and relegated to founder status with not much equity.

The deal terms offered by an angel are there to protect you, not diminish you. These standard clauses and requirements are in place based on best practices in early-stage investing. The terms are structured in recognition of how value is created incrementally. Deal terms reward you for your consistency and loyalty to creating exit value.

Takeaway
So, how bad can it get? If the company runs out of money before it can exit, and the investors are out of dry powder, everyone is going to get crushed. First-time entrepreneurs often exit with less than 10% ownership because they failed to plan.

73

Find subject matter experts and enjoy a payoff at every stage

It helps to surround an entrepreneur with expertise, especially when it's industry-specific, or domain knowledge that helps increase the odds of success. There are two formal ways to engage subject matter experts.

The first is from the investor side. Identify an individual or individuals with subject matter expertise who can help with due diligence. These experts may be a part of your network or within the syndicate of investors. Who knows, they could be a great fit as an independent board member on the deal where they know potential acquirers to accelerate an exit.

The second method is to create a board of advisors for each deal. The entrepreneur may have already started this process and you'll have to determine the strength and engagement of that advisory board during due diligence. Some may be friends of the entrepreneur and may not have the sophistication required to assist the company moving forward. Some may be listed on an advisory board in name only, but others may be willing to help in more of a hands-on role. An advisory board, while not required, can fill-in the many management gaps often seen in start-up deals.

Advisors may get 0.25% - 1.0% of the company through stock options. While this sounds like a lot, their involvement can provide a significant return on the deal. Advisors give you access to the right people, at the right time, to move a company forward. An advisory board is typically agreed to by the board, but, as an investor, you may require that particular experts are added to support your strategy for the company going forward.

Remember, investors have the right to require or to appoint members to an advisory board. If it is something you want, make sure to include it in the term sheet along with an allocation of stock options to use as incentive.

For the Entrepreneur

You may have assembled an advisory board to help you when you started the company. Advisors can help fill gaps for an entrepreneur with functional expertise (finance, marketing, operations) or domain/industry experience. It really helps when you have someone on your advisory board who is well-known in the industry and can open doors for you.

During the due diligence phase, investors will not only investigate the level of subject matter expertise of your existing advisors, but also explore their commitment level to going forward. Be prepared to change out some advisors with experts recommended from the investor side.

Takeaway
Give away small portions of stock to advisors; you will need their help to get to a quick exit.

Convertible notes have a limited upside

Beware if the entrepreneur asks you to take a convertible note instead of equity. Convertible notes can be deceptive because they do not fully value the risk you are taking as an investor. We recommend that convertible notes only be used by current investors as a bridge between funding rounds.

Too many early-stage investors agree to a convertible note because they don't know how to price the round or because the entrepreneur doesn't want to give away too much of the company before the next inflection point is reached. In practice, when an entrepreneur requires investors to use a convertible note, it could demonstrate that the entrepreneur doesn't value the risk or non-tangible assets that the angel investor is bringing to the table.

If you, as an investor, agree to a convertible note, you will limit your upside potential in the deal. Truthfully, in the event of a major breakthrough, the most you can gain between now and the next round of funding is discount pricing when your note is converted to stock in the next round, typically 5%-30%, and some nominal amount of interest. That potential gain is not commensurate with the level of risk you are accepting.

As a holder of a convertible note, you're not protected in the way you think you are. The discounts and interest may still be negotiable by the next group of investors, and if things aren't going well for the company, even the principal can be negotiated away. Nothing is a sure thing from round to round.

For the Entrepreneur
Angels want preferred stock in recognition of the risk they are taking when they back the potential of your product, identified market and management team.
Entrepreneurs who insist on using convertible notes versus equity may lose the best and most experienced angels; in fact, their deals may not get funded and they won't be able to access the best talent in the board room.

Like an inflated pre-money valuation or seeking an excessive salary to run the company indefinitely, the convertible note sends a clear message to the investor that you don't understand how to create the best conditions for earning an exit. It echoes the founder's belief that investors should put in all the cash, take all the risk, but you will be the only one to gain if things go well.

Entrepreneur Beware: A convertible note can be even more dangerous for you. Some predatory investors will use a convertible note with significant penalties if certain events and payments are not met. These investors will take over your company, leaving you with nothing but a pink slip.

Definition of Convertible Debt

A debt instrument (such as a promissory note) that can be converted to equity of the issuer (either as common stock or preferred stock) at a predetermined discount, with or without nominal interest, in a future round of funding.

75

Quarterly reports should be required and written in the term sheet

The majority of entrepreneurs you'll encounter as a start-up investor are not financial wizards. They're more passionate about starting companies than they are about statistical analysis. Much of what you will contribute as an angel is giving these entrepreneurs some knowledge of financial management to incorporate with their core strengths of innovation, development and marketing. The screening process will most likely give you the first clue to the entrepreneur's level of financial sophistication. If the deal progresses into due diligence, and nobody on the founding team seems capable of reading a financial statement, start to think about whom you can pull in as a board member with strong financial skills and a willingness to be more hands-on during the early stages of the business.

The quarterly financial reports you'll require in the term sheet are a good tool for keeping you and your fellow investors informed. You can take everything learned in due diligence and easily create milestones for the next twelve or twenty-four months, and the inflection points needed to reach an exit. You can manage expectations and performance with a single snapshot and scorecard.

Compiling and distributing a quarterly report to the board is a simple type of milestone. These reports can be easily printed straight out of the company's bookkeeping software, especially since most deals won't require audited financials. Tardiness and errors in reporting should be cause for closer monitoring. You will also be able to determine how coachable and trustworthy your founder is, as you take him through that first set of quarterly reports. Has he manipulated the end-of-quarter numbers somehow? Has he front-loaded or held back financial information? Are there obvious or not-so-obvious omissions? Are there excuses as to why revenue fell short?

If the financial knowledge gap for the founder is mostly educational, step in and help informally. If your board members are preoccupied with other areas of the business, make sure someone is taking the lead as a financial mentor. A strong business strategy can start with a clear understanding of the financials. Note that quarterly reports can be much more than financials. Entrepreneurs should be willing to provide written updates on the business as a whole.

For the Entrepreneur

Quarterly reports create consistency during conversations with your board. By agreeing upon specific financial metrics and ratios, you can quickly gauge how you're progressing. Using a three-month reporting time range allows you to see key trends and spot variances in time to make adjustments.

You'll usually find the requirements for quarterly financial reports in the "Information Rights" section of a term sheet. The expectations will be clearly defined. You might have thirty days (or forty-five days) to provide the financials after the reporting period ends.

One of your angel board members should have a strong financial background. Think of this person as a very expensive Chief Financial Officer who doesn't burden your overhead expense. You may have worked with this individual during due diligence. They're there to support you with budgeting and financial management, as well as to ensure a clean representation of the financials in advance of a sale of your company.

Takeaway

The quarterly financial reports required in the term sheet are the best tools for keeping you and your fellow investors informed. Make sure to hold the entrepreneur's feet to the fire.

76

Certain board members are better for the launch, expansion, or the exit. Replace them at each stage

Successful people with large bank accounts typically have large egos to match. Many of these successful people end up serving on private company boards, but how do you measure their effectiveness? The value of a board member is based on special skillsets to help navigate a company through its lifecycle. Some board members are just better suited to help the company in the very early stages of a start-up, helping to raise capital or setting up controls and metrics; whereas, other board members may be better for growth stage companies, creating value and negotiating exits. For the most part, it's difficult to clearly explain this to board members of your various portfolio companies. Everyone, due to the nature of the position, feels that he is doing everything possible to get the business to a profitable exit.

Remember, most early deals will have a five person board, typically consisting of two founders, two investors, and one independent board member with direct industry experience relating to the business. While many deals will automatically include terms for the lead investor to control the investor seats, it is important, as a co-investor in the deal, to make sure that the best possible people are appointed to those positions at each stage of the company's development. Again, you need to leverage the board's contribution by having board members in place who are appropriate resources for each stage of the company, from the day it launches to the day it exits. If you think this won't happen, you should reconsider making an investment in the deal.

Some investors may be serial entrepreneurs who are really strong working with start-ups, understanding customer needs and developing marketing plans. As the company grows and enters a higher growth phase that consumes more capital and is focused on revenue, you might put other board members in place that can help raise bank debt, build out distribution channels or help establish a formal sales organization. As the company nears an exit, you and the founder will need to rely on board members who are experienced at identifying and communicating with potential acquirers and investment bankers. Make sure the term sheet includes details on how board seats are voted on. If you think the timing for an exit is quicker than normal, make sure to have a conversation about the board with your syndication partners and the entrepreneur. You may need to have potential board members for the expansion and exit stages already observing board meetings to make for a smoother transition. It takes time to get comfortable with new board members; don't let that delay the company's progress.

For the Entrepreneur

Consider how your company has already evolved from the seed stage. You began with an idea, developed a prototype, bootstrapped, found a market, tested the product on potential customers and perhaps brought on other team members. Each phase required different skills sets and experience, yet you were able to navigate through each phase successfully.

Now that the company is potentially worth more and you're seeking to attract outside funding, the next phases of growth will require more capital, business acumen, direct industry experience and contacts. This is where your expert board will help you become more aligned with your exit strategy. The two original investor board members will more than likely change over this time period to bring the appropriate expertise to the company at the appropriate phase of development. From a support standpoint, you'll actually be doubling or tripling the number of resources that you can tap as you head toward your first exit.

Takeaway
As you screen and conduct due diligence on a deal, begin thinking about who the most appropriate board members might be for each of the stages of the company. Start-up, growth, and exit will each require different skill sets. Good board members know when it's time to step aside.

77

Board members should get compensated for their time

Most early-stage companies do not have the capital to provide cash compensation to board members. That being the case, the start-up will often need to compensate the board with a strong stock option program. You most likely have friends who serve on public boards or you know of someone who is compensated for serving on a board. Being on a board does not automatically require compensation; however, if independent board members are getting compensated, then the investor board seats should expect to also be compensated.

At a minimum, board members should be compensated for their time and travel. It might be appropriate for you to set an hourly fee for board meeting attendance. Another angel group or angel resource group should be able to help you determine that amount for early-stage companies.

In terms of non-cash compensation, stock options for board members are traditionally issued in the amount of 0.25%-2% of the start-up company, vesting over three to four years. This is a great incentive for engaging board members and allowing them to mentor and open up their network to help the founder move the company toward a lucrative exit, creating liquidity and cash value for those board options.

Where compensation becomes interesting is when you need to replace board members as the company progresses through the growth curve (some board members are better suited for different stages of the company). The first board members wonder what will happen to their shares if they are replaced. Plan in advance for these possibilities, and have the original options issued with clear vesting schedules so as to remove any doubts.

For the Entrepreneur

Providing a strong board to support company growth and to ensure an exit is one of the key attributes of angel investing. These are not your traditional corporate boards that review financial reports and sip water from crystal glasses in a wood-paneled board room. Your board members take a hands-on approach and they will be taking what was discussed and refined during due diligence and driving those key ideas from your pitch and business plan forward. This is about realizing the promise of what you shared with them and leveraging that pre-money valuation. This is about making it real.

Boards will mentor you and members of your team in general business management skills, in areas of finance and execution of the plan. They will provide networking in your industry, far beyond any market research or contacts you have developed so far. Board members get doors opened and phone calls returned on your behalf. Compensation for these services is common and usually a lot cheaper than hiring full-time salaried employees to your team.

> **Takeaway**
> Treat investing as a professional activity. You are not a volunteer. You are taking the risk and deserve to be compensated for your time when it is appropriate and reasonable.

78

You don't always need a CEO right away

Sometimes you are presented with a deal where the founder is operationally and technically focused, but lacks the overall vision and drive to push all facets of the company forward. Depending on the deal, it can be advantageous to keep him focused on a particular area versus spreading his abilities across too many issues. Yet, because of that decision, the time to reach an exit may be delayed; the founder is so deliberate and always wants every single item and aspect to be perfect. He may not understand that hitting a milestone on time, with less-optimal components or materials, may be more important than perfection. We recommend that an entrepreneur like this should be paired with someone in an Executive Chairman role: someone senior, who advises the founder and provides a form of "adult supervision" to a young company.

An Executive Chairman can be expensive. He might get anywhere from 2-10% of the company; however, paying an executive chairman with stock does cost less than recruiting a new CEO to work full-time with the founders and current management team. There is also a trade-off because the Executive Chairman is not a full-time position. The board will need to monitor the chairman's schedule and contribution to ensure the entrepreneur is getting the support he needs.

Recruiting an Executive Chairman can be relatively easy. Individuals who fit this role could be an "Entrepreneur in Residence" at a local university's business school or a recently exited entrepreneur who is not sure what direction to take next. Successful entrepreneurs and others with early-stage company experience are looking for these kinds of roles because it allows them to engage with a company without a full-time commitment. However, make sure you interview a number of candidates before making a decision. Personalities, background, and previous industry knowledge can be highly important.

For the Entrepreneur

Getting to an exit is all about balancing skill sets, experience and talent. You may have a technical or operational background, or maybe you are very talented in areas like marketing and sales. A growth company needs experience on many levels, with the primary skill being the ability to strategically move the business forward to an acquisition on an accelerated timeline.

In addition to board monitoring, your investors may want to bring in someone in an Executive Chairman role to promote success, and that person may need to be compensated with a significant amount of stock options. Be flexible when investors tap additional resources to benefit your company. While the chairman may only be involved part-time, be prepared for a significant impact to the company from his contribution.

Takeaway
Pair an Executive Chairman with a technical founder to help drive your portfolio company toward an exit. Executive chairmen are expensive (in terms of stock), but worth the cost.

79

Take educational seminars on how to be a better investor and board member

Sure, time is money and you hate sitting in a room listening to educational seminars, but have you finished learning everything you'd like to learn as a start-up investor? Do you really know all the rules and best practices of the industry? Even if you know enough, learning the current trends from investors across the country should help create better opportunities for potentially higher returns. It might be difficult at this stage in your career to jump into investment banking or venture capital, and why would you want to? Angel investing is one area where you can learn the ropes from other people's mistakes. Why not spend some quality time with your peers and exchange war stories?

As an accredited investor, you are immediately part of a learning community, no matter where you live in the country. By associating with other angels and syndicating and vetting deals with other groups, you benefit from informal mentoring from your peers and co-investors. Your input and insights will be considered as you test your assumptions across all deals, and you may be especially valuable if your industry experience aligns with the specific market that a common portfolio company is pursuing.

We encourage you to formally participate in courses offered by national groups such as the Angel Resource Institute, an organization – founded by the Ewing Marion Kauffman Foundation and leaders of angel groups in the United States and Canada – devoted to providing education, training, and information on best practices in the field of angel investing. Typical programs from these groups include on-site, full-day seminars and workshops offered in different regions of the country, as well as webinars and podcasts. Most of the above are individual or panel formats taught by successful angels. Topics include term sheets, due diligence, company valuation, exits and portfolio strategy, as well as working with founders and boards after the investment is made. Case studies figure prominently in these courses and networking with fellow participants is strongly encouraged. You may gain additional deal flow and co-investors for a future syndication. If you're interested in starting a formal group in your region, there are courses offered specifically to help support you, too. Make your experience with angel investing fun, and never stop learning from others.

For the Entrepreneur

Start-ups involve large amounts of leverage. You've taken seed funds from your savings, from family and friends, and developed a working prototype, identified a market and possibly booked revenue. Now that you are at the stage of considering angel investing, your company is still considered a highly risky investment. You can mitigate that risk by leveraging with many different angel-related resources. One single angel, with decades of business experience and a large network of contacts, represents exponential growth potential for your company. Now combine that angel with other angels in a group, a fund or a syndicate of funds. Lastly, add the professional infrastructure that now exists in national angel investing associations. Many of these larger groups offer educational programs for both angels and entrepreneurs. Make sure your angel is plugged in and taking advantage of these resources to help you grow your company.

Takeaway
Discover the various courses that are available to you, as investors and entrepreneurs, from the Angel Resource Institute. Contact ARI for more information at angelresourceinstitute.org.

80

It's okay to use warrants

It's important to first understand the definition of a warrant. A warrant is a security, similar to stock options for non-employees, that gives the holder the right to buy shares of common stock in the company at an agreed to price. The warrant typically has an expiration date of one to ten years, depending on its original purpose. Many angel investors request warrants if they are taking on some additional risk. Maybe they are funding a bridge round or doing a short-term loan to fund an unexpected expense that the company failed to plan for.

Warrants are also used by debt holders and service providers. Debt holders, specifically venture banks, will use warrants as a way to capitalize, not only on the upside of a deal, but as a means to keep interest rates competitive with traditional banks despite the higher risk of funding an early-stage business. Many venture banks require investments by Venture Capital funds before committing to a deal; although, with fewer venture funds in the market, some venture banks have started to relax that requirement.

In terms of service providers, early-stage companies have used warrants as a way to pay for reduced professional fees. There are some law firms that will take a percentage of their fees in warrants to help a start-up company preserve cash. In general, warrants work fairly well.

Unfortunately, the issue with warrants is managing them on the capitalization table. Too many companies fail to disclose outstanding warrants. A warrant will dilute ownership and must be disclosed. As an investor, make sure to ask questions about warrants during due diligence and make sure that information is included in a term sheet before making an investment.

Note: The use of "penny warrants," with an exercise stock price of $0.01, is becoming common practice in certain parts of the country as a mechanism to penalize a company if certain milestones are not met in a timely manner. For the most part, investor groups, who are required to provide their members with tax statements, will implement terms in the closing documents that require the company to provide warrants if their tax documents are not prepared and forwarded to the investor group by a certain date. These groups do not want to have all of their members file tax extensions because a single portfolio company could not provide information on time.

For the Entrepreneur

Help the investors in due diligence. Be forthright and honest. If there are issues or items from the earlier stage of the company, bring those to light immediately. Disclose any warrants that might be associated with a debt or previous funding rounds that could create a dilution issue for new investors. Remember to disclose warrants issued to service providers; they are a great way to pay for service fees.

You want to do everything possible to be cooperative during due diligence. Some experienced angels and those who syndicate may actually have a fairly rapid process because they are able to spread out the workload or have seen enough deals to eliminate non-starters and put all their attention on deals with potential. Still, you don't want to be the one slowing the due diligence process. Think of it as one of the many milestones you need to hit on the way to getting funded.

Takeaway
Before investing, make sure the capitalization table includes outstanding warrants. If exercised, warrants will dilute your ownership percentage. Warrant (also known as a "Stock Warrant"): Securities that give stockholders the right, but not the obligation to buy shares of common stock at a fixed price over a specified period of time. Warrants are similar to stock options and offered to investors (or to service providers in exchange for fees.)

Definition of Penny Warrant
Similar to a warrant in that these are securities that give the holder the right, but not the obligation, to buy shares of the company over a given period of time. However, the strike price is set at $.01.

81

Always vest a portion of the founder's shares

Did you ever buy a new car? If so, do you remember how nice the salesperson was while she was trying to close the deal? A few days later when you are having a minor issue with the car, you call that favorite salesperson for help. Guess what? She's not bending over backwards to help you now. She's moved on to the next customer, leaving you stuck navigating the dealership to find someone else who can help. Well, start-ups can be very similar to this experience. You fund a deal, and the entrepreneur, you thought was going to run the company for the next five years, decides to leave to take on another start-up venture. Now what? Investors need to find a replacement and, oh yeah, the company needs to issue more stock to get the new person on board. You just got diluted! So how do you stop this?

To limit the risk of losing key leaders of a new portfolio company after an investment, angels should require, in the term sheet, that the founders and key personnel vest their shares over an agreed-to period of time. You want to ensure against them leaving the company to pursue other interests. If they do leave, the company needs to be able to recapture those shares in order to incent new employees to join the company and keep it moving forward.

A typical vesting schedule would be over three or four years with some portion of the stock vested today and the remainder divided evenly over an agreed-to period of time. Of course, if an exit occurs during this period, all shares would immediately vest and the employees would benefit fully from the sale. Truthfully, this is a difficult conversation because employees feel that they have already earned those shares. Any pushback should be considered a sign that the team is not fully behind the company or has already started to look for its next engagement.

There can be some flexibility in this rule; however, it involves lowering the pre-money valuation and creating a larger option pool for future employees. You really need to use this as a negotiating term when structuring the deal. It is important to note that some investors prefer the use of redemption rights for founder shares. Redemption will allow the company to buy back a predetermined percentage of its outstanding shares at a nominal amount from the entrepreneur or team member who left the company. In theory, both mechanisms work well.

For the Entrepreneur

Many of the deal terms you see involve protecting investors for the risks they are taking and most likely these are areas where they have been burned previously. A stock vesting schedule for founders and key employees is one of the terms. If you leave to start another company, the agreement with an angel will prohibit you or your management team from walking away with all of your stock. That stock will be needed for the executives that replace you. Investors do not want to make a risky investment that is primarily based on backing you and your team with money and then have everyone decide to leave the company; essentially allowing you to profit by rolling the dice on a potential return in the future. It's not fair to the investor.

> **Takeaway:**
> **Vesting Founders' Shares Schedule**
> Key personnel may be required to vest their original shares, over a defined period of time, in a company when the first institutional round of investment is received. Typically the time period is three to four years and is fully-vested upon a liquidation event. The goal of vesting founders' shares is to keep key personnel engaged with the company.

82

Make sure to include liquidation preferences; it's fair to everyone

You deserve to know when and how you will get paid on your investment from these deals. Investing with an exit as an end-game requires an understanding of generally accepted liquidation concepts and tools. Given the high risk, there are standard measures and metrics in place that govern how you will benefit when the company is sold. This not only establishes a level playing field for accredited investors, it's a way to communicate early on with the company founders to create alignment and manage expectations.

To start, you expect to be paid first (if there is not enough money to go around). A standard way to protect your interests is with a liquidation preference clause in the term sheet. Liquidation preference defines both the sequence and the amount distributed. In the simplest terms, you will be paid a multiple on your original investment made in exchange for the preferred stock. The liquidation preference clause in the term sheet and any funding agreements specifically define how much money the investors will realize from the company upon exit, ahead of the founders and investors in previous rounds. Your preferred shares are compensated in full prior to any payment to common shares held by ordinary shareholders prior to liquidation.

Secondly, when you have a participating liquidation preference, this means you receive common stock in addition to your original investment in the event the company is sold. This stock is allocated according to your pro rata share in the company.

Liquidation preferences reward you as the angel investor for those instances when the company that you invested in is very successful and attracts an acquirer, but also in the event the company does not perform as well as expected. These liquidation preferences also represent tools for communicating and negotiating with the company founders to determine an equitable arrangement, including the pre-money valuation. Caution: if the multiple on the liquidation preference is too high, entrepreneurs may not be incentivized to exit if the deal does not provide them with any proceeds. Negotiating the right balance is needed to keep all investors and management team members aligned and focused on a quick exit.

INVESTOR PERSPECTIVE

For the Entrepreneur

Your investors are taking the financial risk and the standard term sheet will reward them first when the company is sold. A standard liquidation preference amount is 1x of the original investment. You don't want to be so desperate to get the deal funded that you allow your investors to have a higher liquidation preference of 2-3x (or more). Most investors will also require "participating preferred" rights to get their capital back first and then to participate in the company sale according to their pro rata share.

Remember, you are asking investors to fund your venture without guarantee of return or liquidity. They are putting their personal wealth behind unproven management, unproven market adoption and no market for the stock other than a future sale of the business. For most Series-A rounds, expect to see strong investor preferences. When investors require a participating preferred liquidation, this could allow you negotiation room to seek a higher pre-money valuation.

Definition of Participating Preferred
The right of an investor to first receive capital back when a company is sold, then participate in the sale based upon pro rata share of the common stock.

Definition of Liquidation Preference
Amount repaid to an investor when the company is liquidated, defined as a multiple of capital invested.

83

Understand protective provisions

Angels prefer to take the company all the way to an exit. Even if it takes two or even three rounds to be able to attract an acquirer for the company, angels want to be the ones who anticipate that scenario. They want to direct the terms and what happens on the capitalization table. They don't want to take all the early risk and then have their equity diluted when a venture group comes in at the less-risky stage and crams everyone down. The group with the money writes the rules. Everyone has to accept that or go out of business and take the full loss.

Angels rely on protective provisions in order to maintain some level of control over the life of the deal. Protective provisions will constantly change and are very different across the country. Angels or investors who have been hurt by keeping limited provisions will be more apt to add stronger provisions to each subsequent deal. Entrepreneurs with a track record of success will have fewer provisions.

A typical protective provision in a Series A Convertible Preferred Stock term sheet, currently used by a large number of angel groups, will appear as follows:

Written consent of a least a majority of Series A shares outstanding is required for (i) a merger or consolidation (other than one in which stockholders of the Company own a majority by voting power of the outstanding shares of the surviving or acquiring corporation), (ii) a sale, lease, transfer, or other disposition of all or substantially all of the assets of the Company; (iii) liquidation, dissolution, or winding up of the Company; (iv) amend, alter, or repeal any provision of the Certificate of Incorporation or Bylaws in a manner adverse to the Series A shares; (v) create or authorize the creation of or issue any other security convertible into or exercisable for any equity security, having rights, preferences, or privileges senior to or on parity with the Series A, or increase the authorized number of shares of Series A; (vi) purchase or redeem or pay any dividend on any capital stock prior to the Series A; or (vii) create or authorize the creation of any debt security, unless such debt security has received the prior approval of the Board of Directors, including the approval of a majority of Series A Directors; or (viii) increase or decrease the size of the Board of Directors.

INVESTOR PERSPECTIVE

As an investor, are you comfortable allowing a majority vote on a liquidation event, or would you like to require that you have to also approve a sale? Make sure you understand the implications of each provision and how it may affect getting to a quick exit.

For the Entrepreneur

While many terms may appear unfair to you as the founder, protective provisions are established to prevent certain events from occurring that could otherwise open you up for liability. Let's face it; you needed the money to drive the company forward. You need to be fair and open with the investors. In general, you may work with the investor to define what it takes to approve certain events that will impact ownership, fundraising and the exit. As discussed elsewhere in this book, sometimes provisions may be less onerous, but angels have learned from mistakes trusting other entrepreneurs and they don't want to repeat history.

Definition of Protective Provisions
Allows certain shareholders to veto certain actions, such as selling the company or raising additional rounds of capital or changing the number of board members. They can protect the preferred minority shareholders (typically the angel investors) from unfair actions by the common majority (founders).

84

Hands-on angel investor: monitor progress with the term sheet

As an angel, you might think your responsibilities diminish after screening, due diligence, negotiating terms and closing the deal. You may have assigned other board members to the deal, and you're ready to diversify your portfolio with another deal or two. Not so fast.

You could be facing a crisis, or at least some form of drifting behavior, almost immediately. You'll need to keep a close watch on the deal at the beginning to give yourself the extra assurance that your new portfolio company is staying on the agreed-upon course. Even a brief, informal check-in with the founder is permissible and helpful. You want him to know you are always close by.

You'll want to keep the term sheet handy and stay familiarized with the key clauses because you may need to act swiftly and with the authority the documents give you. Here are some of the subtle and not-so-subtle warning signs that could prompt your attention and a review of key documents: tardiness of any kind, including payments or reports; large or numerous small variances on financial statements; a pattern of footnotes to financials with elaborate explanations; thefts of property or inventory; drama among personnel; staff turnover or inability to hire key staff members; unresponsive founder or staff; frequent vacations or off-site meetings at resorts.

You may even notice after a while a certain hesitation or reluctance of board members to talk about the business, or frustration on the part of the founder as it relates to the board members. You may need to convene your team in order to make a quick remedy, and it always helps to cite the term sheet and closing documents.

You'll want deal documents handy as you reach any phase of stock vesting or looking at potential acquirers for an exit. It will have been several years since the closing, so you will want to make sure everyone has a fresh look at what was agreed upon. Exits can be a stressful time for the founder, so having your documents on hand can keep any discussions focused objectively on the key terms.

For the Entrepreneur

Once the deal has closed with your angel or angel group, your natural inclination is to file the documents away in a safe place. Unfortunately, that can be dangerous. It will be easy to drift from what you have agreed to accomplish. The term sheet and closing documents summarize the key governance and navigation tools you'll need to grow value and achieve an exit.

You should understand every clause and metric in the term sheet, and commit it to memory. Or post a summary of it in a prominent place so you can review it often. You want to be more on top of this than the angel. You want to own the numbers and provide answers before you are asked to. This builds confidence and allows your board to concentrate on higher-priority items for the company.

Takeaway
Referring to the closing terms of the deal is a good resource to keep the entrepreneur focused and engaged with investors. An entrepreneur is no longer able to act without approval from the board or his investors.

85

Understand majority approval versus super majority

Board control does not equate to the percentage of ownership. You and your co-investors will typically take 20-40% of a start-up's equity in a Series-A funding round; you aren't necessarily interested in taking a controlling interest. Even if a second or third round of investment is needed to advance the company closer to an exit, your preferred stock may still represent less than 50% of the company. Your strategy as an investor is not to control the deal, but to limit as much risk as possible on the deal until you exit. You don't want to be the majority shareholder, nor do you want to be the one running the company as CEO. You're building a portfolio, after all.

Yet you do want to be able to exert your influence and protect your interests. The corporate statute or certificate of incorporation will define your full and class voting rights. With full voting rights, you vote as if your preferred shares have been converted to common shareholders on each matter. In terms of class voting rights, preferred stock votes as a single class or combined with all preferred stock rounds, on certain matters such as the sale of the company or the election of board members.

As a minority shareholder, assuming you own less than 50% of the deal, you will want protection against risky actions of the majority owners (including the founder) and the management team. Standard in any deal and documented in the term sheet will be special voting rights or supermajority approval. With these rights, you'll be able to step in as minority shareholders and take action. Triggering events could include failure to meet milestones, large variances to quarterly or annual projections, loss of key employees or anything that threatens the direction of the company. Once you understand how special voting rights are structured, have a conversation with the founder to make sure he can accept this arrangement.

INVESTOR PERSPECTIVE

For the Entrepreneur

While angels are not interested in controlling your company, they do want to be able to protect against events or decisions that pose a threat to their investment. This might include the purchase of unnecessary assets, acquiring another company or a poorly structured contract or licensing deal that significantly over-commits current resources. A series of financial losses or resignation of a key management could also trigger board action.

Make sure you understand the difference between equity ownership and voting rights. Even though you own the majority of the equity, the term sheet will spell out special voting rights accorded to the board to protect investors. Again, the board and investors do not want to run the company. They want to guide it to a series of inflection points where it can be acquired and they can get their pay day.

> **Takeaway**
> Majority stock ownership does not mean that the entrepreneur makes all the decisions. Investors have rights, as defined in the deal documents.

86

Let boards make some of the important decisions, but stay informed

You don't have to be on the board of your portfolio company to be a good investor. If you invest in a deal but are not a board member, it is important to take a step back and give the board the authority and autonomy to build a solid relationship with the founder and the management team. There will be plenty of time and opportunity for you to get engaged with the company.

While you may not be part of the formal board monitoring process, you will be able to add value as the business evolves. You may be the one who first met the founder at a networking event, or you led the screening phase or due diligence process. You may represent the strongest source of "institutional memory" regarding the deal. Your unique role might be very helpful if things suddenly go wrong, if there is a major dispute between founders and investors, or when the company is approaching an exit.

You could be valuable when financial reports are shared back to the group from the board; look for details from due diligence that relate specifically to a question about the income statement or balance sheet.

Even with your informal role, you will want to stay involved to provide occasional advice to the business or to support the board and founder. While the independent board member will most likely have the deep industry knowledge and extensive market contacts, you may have functional experience in sales, manufacturing, human resources or operations to support the growth of the company's management team. Even infrequent and informal mentoring could be a factor in keeping communication open with founders.

By staying informed, you will also be able to step in on short notice if needed. The company might encounter an unforeseen problem only you can solve, a board member might need to be replaced, or if the founder "goes rogue" you might be the most likely candidate to take on a leadership role. Being a good investor means paying attention and offering help and coaching as needed.

For the Entrepreneur

You'll work with more individuals in an angel deal than you might with a venture capital investment. You might meet one group of "scout" angels at a conference, deal with a separate group or an angel fund manager during screening and a new set of angels for due diligence. When you are funded, you will have three new board members, two of them specifically appointed by the angel syndicate, and an independent board member that the investors help arrange.

You can count every one of these hands-on angels as part of your new network. While you will have more extensive, scheduled and formal contact with your board members, remember that they may be substituted at times when other angels can provide more specialized assistance. You may also have ongoing interaction with non-board members who will just want to check in with you on occasion. These can be valuable relationships despite their informality.

.

Takeaway
Understand the ethical and fiduciary responsibilities of your appointed board members. If a board member is relatively inexperienced, give him the tools to get educated on what it takes to be an effective board member.

87

Your attorney fees should be paid by the entrepreneur

Closing an early-stage deal is not difficult. In fact, most early-stage deals are comparatively consistent in terms of documentation. There will be a standard set of closing documents that an angel group uses, or that you can get access to through your attorney. Many of the items and stipulations for a closing will have already been covered in discussions and will follow what is stated in the term sheet. If you use a standard term sheet, there is no reason to think the deal will get overly complicated.

A typical closing will include a Term Sheet, Preferred Stock Purchase Agreement, Amended and Restated Articles of Incorporation, Investors Rights Agreement, Capitalization Table, Employment Agreements, Shareholder Consents, Board of Directors Consents, Stock Option Plan (if applicable) and a Form D filed with the Securities and Exchange Commission (SEC). While Form D is not necessarily a requirement, it may be suggested by your attorney.

The attorney fees for the entrepreneur and the investors' group are negotiable and typically total no more than $10,000-$15,000 for a start-up or early-stage deal. Your attorney fees for reviewing the documents and the term sheet should be paid out of the investment proceeds; in other words, they should come out of the portfolio company's freshly enlarged pocket. Angels aren't using other people's money. They are investing their own funds in the company and consider the closing documents a part of the transaction. Keeping a budget for both parties lowers expenses and keeps everyone aligned.

The primary language used in the term sheet is: "Company counsel to draft closing documents; company to pay all legal and administrative costs of the financing at Closing, including reasonable fees (not to exceed $X,000) and expenses of Investor counsel." If there are multiple investors in the round, they will need to determine how to allocate the fee reimbursement.

For the Entrepreneur

Always keep your focus on the end-game: the exit. There is an implicit imbalance with a start-up because relatively little tangible value has been created yet. Numerous protections are in place for investors. It may appear they're getting the better part of the deal as you review a term sheet. Don't forget that they are assuming most of the risk and putting in most of the cash that you need to make the company successful.

To protect yourself, you should conduct due diligence on potential investors. Before you approach an individual angel or group, make sure they have a reputation for dealing with entrepreneurs openly and honestly. Make sure they won't take undue advantage of your need for capital. Make sure there are caps on certain expenses like legal fees and other financial arrangements that could expose you. Good investors will be reasonable.

> **Takeaway**
> Early-stage investors should consider the fees associated with the closing documents to be a part of their investment. Make sure to include these in the term sheet.

RULES THAT HELP INVESTORS & ENTREPRENEURS GET TO A SUCCESSFUL EXIT

ENTREPRENEUR PERSPECTIVE

88

Keep founders hungry for an exit

Don't imagine entrepreneurs sitting at home without food in their refrigerator; that's not the plan. Rather, provide a roadmap for the entrepreneur to envision the wealth and freedom that will come the day after their company is sold. You want the entrepreneur to be motivated for the end game, not the job. Make sure your founder wants a big payday versus a paycheck. Why? Because you typically don't get a payday until the company has a liquidation event. You want to keep the entrepreneur focused on the exit, so don't pay him too much to start.

Think about a scenario where the company has been fairly successful, but not to the degree that would interest potential acquirers; however, because of the company's success, the compensation package for the entrepreneur has exploded. The board's compensation committee jumped executive salaries up to industry comparables and recently instituted cash bonuses to the founder for hitting yearly profit targets. What's wrong with this picture? Well, the executive team and entrepreneur are getting rich, but you aren't. Your money is stuck in a private company that is becoming more of a lifestyle business than a growth story. This causes a big disconnect between you and the entrepreneur.

So how can you avoid this scenario? How can you use the term sheet to protect against this? It's fairly simple: add redemption rights or a forced buyback into the funding agreement. The driving factor is protection for the investors. If, after a defined number of years, a liquidation event does not occur, the investors have the right to force the company to purchase their shares at a pre-determined multiple. Investors will typically have the option to exercise this right, and typically it is only exercised if investors no longer have faith in the management team. Realistically, in many of these cases, the company will not have the capital to make the payment and, as a result, will be in default. A default may (if the documents are properly drafted) allow the investor to take additional steps including the option of forcing the firm to liquidate. This is not good for either party and could kill a company. As an investor, you are partially at fault for allowing the salary to creep up.

While you have the knowledge to use redemption rights in your term sheet, it is more important to know how to keep this from happening in the first place. Have an active board compensation committee to monitor the financial status of the business and to keep salaries in line. Provide enough of a salary to put a roof over the heads of the management team, but not enough to make them complacent, and beware of founders who push too hard on the salary issue. Founders look at what the potential exit means to them versus several years of guaranteed salary. Remember, you put your money into the deal, you took a big financial risk, and you don't get a salary out of the business. Keep founders hungry for an exit. It shouldn't be about an entrepreneur's lifestyle before the sale, but instead, what it can be post-sale. It needs to be about getting you a return on your investment.

For the Entrepreneur

Salaries can kill companies. Yes, you do need to make a living, but don't burden a start-up with too much overhead. Your investors' cash is for building and selling the product, not building a great living for yourself.

Before you fundraise, assess your personal budget. See if you and your management team can live on less during the first three to five years of the deal. It's important to keep salary and benefits lower than any of you might expect. It will make it easier to fundraise if the investor sees that your team is making a financial sacrifice as well. Sometimes it may be difficult for you to translate the value of your stock and options on the capitalization table into a real-world figure; however, stock is where real wealth is created.

When investors are ready to exit, you should be aligned with them, regardless of salary and benefits and the security of a steady job. Conversely, you could have investors who decline an exit if they feel the multiple represented is too low. You probably didn't put in any money and you'll want them to take the offer in hand. Make sure you know your investors' expectations.

Definition of Redemption Right
Allows the investor the ability to force the company to liquidate the original investment at a predetermined price if the company does not reach a liquidation event in a specified period of time.

89

Don't be forced to divorce a portfolio company

More than anything, this book targets the core values of strong board involvement: regular communication between founders, management, and investors, and the execution of the business plan to drive a successful and quick exit. If you are able to keep an entrepreneur focused on the end game and willing to work with you to get there, then there is no reason to think you will have issues that necessarily damage relationships. Conversely, if you aren't on speaking terms with the entrepreneurs you funded, then you are probably not seeing the returns needed to be a start-up investor. Leverage your contacts by networking with other early-stage angel investors. What can they do to get the entrepreneur talking to them? Sometimes it just takes a little mediation to get the conversation going again.

As discussed, it's challenging enough to build strong deal flow and a diverse investment portfolio without having to kill a deal after it is already underway. You may come to a point where you no longer have confidence in the founder to run the company or navigate it through a crisis. There may be challenges related to management team members who are personally close to the founder. Make sure, during deal screening and due diligence, you create stressful situations for the founder and observe the reactions when placed under pressure. You'll know if you can trust that individual during the stress of tough times and when the company is close to an exit. If the entrepreneur shuts down, you know the risk profile of the investment just shot through the roof. One of the characteristics of a great entrepreneur is to be an expert at managing stress.

Stress may not be limited to the actions of management but to a market or opportunity that was misread by the team. Maybe, after a wave of roll-ups in the industry that the company was left out of, the business needs to retrench and find other target acquirers.

Remedy what you can as soon as you can so stress does not build up. If something about the company keeps you awake at night, your gut analysis is probably right. Communicate with the founder with a quick informal check-in. If for some reason, you can't see eye-to-eye with the founder, get someone who can be a positive influence on the board with the ability to set the direction of the company.

For the Entrepreneur

We recommend taking as many avoidance measures as possible. Frequently step back after you've received funding and assess how things are going, as if you were an outside board member. Where have the risks potentially increased even with funding? What resources do you need to address the threat? If you think that there is something material to the business that you should communicate with your board formally during a meeting or informally on a quick call, don't hesitate. These are, after all, engaged investors who would like to make it all the way to an exit without the heavy hand and dilution cram-down that bringing in venture capital, especially late to the game, would represent.

You don't want to have to unwind a deal that's already underway. Angel groups are so closely networked these days that it will be impossible to seek funding from this category for years. Word gets around quickly.

Takeaway
Remember, this is the founder's idea, not yours. If you are a typical early stage investor, you've run your own company and are now in a position to make money off of someone else's blood, sweat and tears. Keep your ego in check while checking the founder's vision versus reality.

90

A milestone is only a fact when it's actually reached, not when the entrepreneur says it is

Significant milestones can be a lot of different things for different kinds of companies. Milestones can range from attaining significant revenue for a product company to completing clinical studies for a life science company. Milestones can be small or large. They can signal the success or failure of the company. Milestones can be inflection points, providing a roadmap to an exit. Milestones are designed by entrepreneurs, with the help of investors, to ensure that the company is heading down the right path. In other words, is the strategy working? It's easy for an entrepreneur to steer off-course. Milestones keep all parties focused on a common goal.

In a product company investment, a revenue milestone is what often justifies the pre-money valuation and confirms that there is actually a paying market out there. While it may take a couple of weeks, months, or even years for some start-ups to hit a substantial level of sales, there could be many false hopes along the way. There may be a tendency, by the entrepreneur, to fudge the status of orders to keep investors happy or to ensure another round of funding. As an angel, you don't necessarily want to be happy, you want to see real orders, not potential purchase orders. The founder needs to get the product shipped out the door before you should be happy.

In a life science or technology deal that is pre-revenue, how do you, as an investor, understand where the next value point is? Many early-stage angels invest in pre-revenue deals on the belief that these companies can have significant exits based on relatively small advances in the lab. But will those advances be enough to get an offer from a strategic acquirer? Investors and entrepreneurs need to work together to clearly define the inflection points that increase value. It's critical that milestones are constantly being addressed and reviewed by the founder and the board. As you gain experience as an investor in private companies, you will continue to demand stronger monitoring and metric reporting. Fewer surprises will lead to more profitable exits.

For the Entrepreneur

This is really easy. Set realistic targets and milestones, and shoot straight with your investors. Don't announce the arrival of anything before it actually arrives. If you are not on solid ground, say so. When you are not completely honest, it creates doubt and disappointment. You will need a high level of trust from your board and current investors for those critical times when you need your investors to step up and support you with additional funds. Remember, at the early-stage, you are not dealing with venture capitalists; you will need angel investors to get your product or pre-revenue company launched. Be realistic with milestones and let investors help you reach your goals.

Takeaway
If an entrepreneur tells you something will happen soon, it doesn't count. It's only real when it actually happens. Set realistic milestones focused on an exit.

91

Get involved and talk to your portfolio companies weekly

If you decide to invest as part of an angel group or syndicate, one of the difficult things about having many investors in the deal is that you don't want all of them calling the entrepreneur every week for a status update; he can't run a company while on the phone. Agree to have just one or two investors reach out in a casual way to check-in once a week. It may only be a five-minute call, and the founder may appreciate the informality and may be more open to providing information beyond what is discussed in a formal board setting.

It's just good practice to have a regular check-in with an entrepreneur. You're not calling on behalf of any board or for any particular purpose other than support. Is there anything the founder needs? Can you help with a personal issue? You're building a relationship with the entrepreneur that will be needed when the company goes through difficult periods. The high levels of trust and cooperation between investor and founder are needed when it's time to sell the company and realize your return.

If the founder asks for help, jump in immediately and show why you are a great investor. You may be able to get the founder to open up on an item he thought too trivial for a board member. Perhaps it's a financial, contract-related or human resources issue where your management background allows you to quickly provide an answer or direction. Maybe it's an issue with the board. You may be dealing with a scientific or technologist founder with limited background in marketing, in sales or in collaborating with customers to refine product features and increase adoption.

Perhaps the founder will open up with you about a potential area of concern far ahead of the time he would even consider it consciously for board review. Your informal weekly call might create a forum where the founder becomes comfortable to test ideas and assumptions. Demonstrate why the angel model of support is the right fit for an early-stage company. Pick up the phone and start the dialogue.

For the Entrepreneur

Leadership can be lonely. By taking the helm of a start-up, you will be spending less time with family and friends. You have new responsibilities to worry about. To make matters worse, if the company is growing too quickly or in a different direction than originally conceived, you can isolate members of your team who may have joined the company for reasons (steady salary, allure of a start-up) that could put them at odds with you as stress levels increase.

Take advantage of anyone from the investor group who reaches out to you, even informally. If you do not have a lot of general management experience, seek out investors who complement your gaps of expertise. Learn from them and show them you can leverage their advice and move the company closer to an exit.

Takeaway
If the founder asks for help, jump in immediately. Your background and network can help push the company toward a positive exit.

92

Take money off the table whenever possible

Exits don't come around all the time. Remember, half of angel-backed deals fail to return an investor's original capital and angels only have so much capital to commit to this game. Investors should take every exit opportunity seriously. It might not even be the greatest exit. In fact, it might even be only a 10% or 20% return on your original investment, but you need to consider taking the money off the table whenever you can. This game is about exits, the good ones and the bad ones.

You may have an entrepreneur who has gone rogue on you. Maybe your board monitoring hasn't been as strong as it should have been. Perhaps you've been in the deal for five years and you don't see light at the end of the tunnel. Sometimes you're just ready to give up. If a willing acquirer emerges and wants to buy you out, take the deal and move on to the next one. Remember, get in and get out.

Exits come in many forms. Sometimes they are because of industry consolidation and roll-ups, and sometimes they are mergers. It might not be a complete exit. It could be a situation where your acquirers are highly motivated, or there are private equity companies who are willing to overpay to get a portion of the shares just so they can get their foot in the door to your industry. You are able to take all the capital back out, but still keep a percentage of the company. That's risk mitigation and a decent exit.

Exits reflect well on your reputation and the reputation of your co-investors. You want to have the street credibility to attract those who are looking for success. An investor with a track record of multiple exits will be attractive; entrepreneurs will want to work with you because of your expertise and knowledge of exits. Exits show that an angel or investment group is capable. They can get a founder all the way to the finish line and, as a result, everyone involved will see a nice payday.

For the Entrepreneur

You'll find that angel investors are very opportunistic about exits, even ones that appear to be premature. They understand that exits are rare events and they will act quickly if they believe the right offer is on the table to sell the company. This is a part of the process that may be difficult from your perspective, as founder, to accept or to adapt to if things are going well with your business. In your mind, you can double sales in the next 12 months and get even more money from another buyer. So why take the first deal?

Remember how many ways an exit benefits you as a serial (repeat) entrepreneur. As a first-time entrepreneur, you might exit with 7-10% of the company; but, after a successful exit, the second time around you might exit with 20% or more of the company. Your pre-money valuations and negotiating power increases on future deals. You now have more knowledge. Your ability to build a company becomes easier and the cost is lower. You may not have to find your next group of investors; they'll find you. Start-up investors understand the risk of not taking the first offer. Some of the intrinsic value of the offer may already assume that your company will hit certain revenue figures. Do you want to delay the exit and take on the risk of actually hitting it?

Takeaway
If your portfolio company is lucky enough to get an offer to sell, take the deal and move on. Success often leads to more success.

93

Investments are illiquid; don't expect to get your money back any time soon

Congratulations on making that first angel investment! You are now voluntarily sentenced to five or more years (perhaps less if you are let out early for good investor-behavior) of volunteerism with your portfolio company. We hope you enjoy each other's company. Whether you have preferred shares, warrants or you have negotiated special considerations, what you do not have is liquidity. You may have scrutinized the deal down to the last detail, but regardless of how much due diligence you conducted, your money is locked in that company until an exit occurs. Get accustomed to it; you're handcuffed to this deal for the next half a decade.

This is why exit-designed angel investing is essential. You won't be able to free-up your money to put into other deals unless you have exits. It's imperative that you and your investing partners are in absolute alignment with the goals of the company. Does everyone support a quick exit? What level of dry powder is committed to see the company through to an exit?

So much depends on your relationship and communication with the founder. You don't want that founder going rogue. You don't want the founder growing complacent with job security and reliant on his salary. You not only want a passionate founder motivated by growth and value creation in a market, you also want a founder who is as motivated as you are to exit. You want board members who are engaged and able to specialize at certain stages of the deal. You want an independent board member who knows the space better than anyone else. It takes a full team to get a company across the finish-line.

When the deal is ready to exit, find the right investment banker to assist the board with the direction and strategy to get it sold. Once sold, it's time to find another deal for your portfolio.

For the Entrepreneur

When angels invest in your company, they will not be able to get their money out whenever they please. They understand that it may take several years, at a minimum, and, as accredited investors, they realize there is no active market for the stock they hold in your company. Liquidity can only come about when there is an exit. It is essential that you, as the founder, not only increase the value of the company, but demonstrate the willingness to create a successful exit.

On the positive side, illiquidity creates an incentive for angels to work with you, to mentor you, to provide access to their experience and networks, to put in place helpful board members specialized in each phase of growth, and in most cases, securing an independent board member with deep knowledge that relates directly to the markets you plan to serve.

Takeaway
Stock in an early-stage company is typically illiquid; an investor has limited ability to resell. Most investors understand an exit event may take five or more years.

94

Don't back entrepreneurs into a corner; a wounded animal can be dangerous

Did you ever see a vein in an entrepreneur's forehead violently pulsate? How many neurons got triggered in your brain after detecting an emotional outburst from the board chairman? If you are in this business long enough, you are going to see arguments and disagreements between investors and founders quite often. When money is involved, emotions easily fly. The trick is knowing when to walk away and fight another day. It's easy, as an investor, to tell an entrepreneur, "don't ever call me again! I am tired of the stories and lack of progress." But that doesn't solve anything. You aren't helping the situation and, in fact, you may have adversely impacted your ability to get your money back. Who's going to run the company if the entrepreneur quits?

As a test case, let's say a portfolio company is having difficulty making payroll, it's Christmas Eve and you get a desperate phone call from the entrepreneur asking for money (it's always Christmas Eve urgency when someone needs extra funds for payroll.) Five minutes ago you were more concerned about wrapping gifts for the kids and drinking with friends at the holiday party. Now your night is ruined and in addition to being mad at the entrepreneur, you are irate that the board and current monitoring reports didn't detect this possibility weeks or months before. What are your options? The founder is telling you to fund the payroll or he is shutting down the company. As an investor, you want to tell the entrepreneur to pound sand and call someone else. But guess what? You are the only investor. Do you back the founder into a corner and refuse to fund until certain milestones or objectives are reach? Or do you fund it and wait until next week to discover what went wrong?

If you begin withholding funds until certain conditions are met, effectively putting the founder on a short leash, he is no longer incentivized to move the company forward. If you switch to a week-by-week monitoring, the founder will look for ways to meet your short-term conditions, but at what expense? He will ignore what you really want him to do in the long term, which is grow the company and sell it. The founder will do everything possible to meet the next set of conditions; you'll have someone selling off the furniture just to meet the financial target.

Challenging an entrepreneur relates back to who has control of the company and whether founders are open to coaching and receiving direction from a board. Did you scrutinize the founder enough in due diligence? We recommend testing founders more during due diligence to see how they will react. Once the money is in the bank, they will act differently. When you back them into a corner, fight or flight, most people in this space are going to fight. Then are you willing to run the company?

For the Entrepreneur

As founder, you're used to having a large degree of control over the company. You are the one most identified with its success and, in the early stages, you are the majority shareholder. As you consider growing the business through an angel round, or any kind of outside investment, you should assess whether you have the willingness to be coached and willingness to let others direct you in order to achieve a common goal. There will be times when your energy, intelligence and leadership will not be enough to get the job done; you'll be subject to working with your investors, and board, to avert a crisis. Make sure this is acceptable.

Takeaway
It's a fine line between coaching and monitoring and overtly controlling the company. Communicate with the entrepreneur and seek alignment on the key objectives. If the entrepreneur won't comply, you may need to use diplomacy.

95

100% of nothing is nothing

Do you know why so many start-up companies fail? It's because the management team is incapable of getting it to the next level. Whether it's a result of failing to raise enough capital to support operations or failing to plan the milestones that lead to an exit, the fact is, something went wrong with the business; the entrepreneur who started with 100% of the deal now has nothing. As an investor, you need to learn how to spot the warning signs of an entrepreneur who doesn't understand that owning 100% of nothing is nothing.

For entrepreneurs, it's a difficult decision to sell equity for funding; they don't like giving up ownership and they definitely don't like giving up control. Some of them overestimate their own ability to succeed and they overvalue the business. Most undervalue both the tangible and intangible assets that angel investors and groups bring to the table. So how do you spot the good entrepreneurs from the bad ones?

Ask questions. Don't be afraid to challenge the motivations of the entrepreneur when he comes to you for funding. Did he wait too long to seek funding and now competitors are creeping into the market? Does he want an active board, or do you get the impression that he wants to make all the decisions? Does he understand what makes the company valuable to a potential acquirer? Is he paying himself too much money and not really caring about an exit?

Statistically, from our experience, a first time entrepreneur will exit with less than 10% of the equity in his business. A lot of this is due to inflated pre-money valuations in the seed-stage and first round of funding, followed by a series of cram-down rounds. Some of this can be avoided if the entrepreneur seeks strong investors early in the process and allows them to help guide the company to a quick exit. While 10% seems like a low number when compared to the original ownership percentage, it is a whole lot better than 100% of a failed business. Help coach the entrepreneur and create an environment to strike a fair deal.

For the Entrepreneur

The capitalization table should be one of your main go-to documents throughout every stage of the deal. Understanding how the "cap" table evolves with each round of funding can provide objective insight and perspective to every decision you make or consider. For example, before you approached the angel investor, you and your early shareholders owned 100% of the company. You may have put cash in, but without a willing buyer, your full ownership would still be worth nothing. You need money from investors to grow the business, to hit revenue growth targets, and to meet other milestones. The point is to get the deal done under reasonable terms and with resources that will help create value an acquirer will pay for at exit.

Takeaway
The entrepreneur needs your cash to grow the business. Remember, the risk of investing is high so you should expect a significant return on your investment when the company is sold.

96

Expect the "I don't have enough in the bank to make payroll next week" call

Remember this scenario? It has happened to us a few more times than we care to remember. Your weekend or a holiday is starting and you receive a call from an entrepreneur that inevitably ends up at: "There's not enough money in the bank to meet payroll." Your immediate action is to ask what the heck happened, but asking the question doesn't solve the immediate issue at hand.

As an investor, you want to make sure the company continues to move forward, assuming you still like the deal. What can you do today to solve the issue? Do you give in and extend more capital short-term? At what terms? Do you throw the problem back to the CEO to solve, asking him to squeeze out more cash by accelerating collections or slowing down payments to suppliers? If you do step in, how do you coach the CEO to make sure it doesn't happen again? You have to let him know that you can't get to an exit if too much time is spent plugging holes. It's distracting from the progress.

In most cases, the entrepreneur should get the board involved first. An emergency funding plan with approved terms will need to be in-place before an additional investment can be made. Don't just write a check as a short-term solution. This is very expensive money and you have every right to set the terms you feel are appropriate for the risk. You don't want the entrepreneur or the board continuously failing to plan, knowing you are willing to step in at the last minute to fund a deficit; and you definitely don't want to do it for free! Keep in mind that you are most likely not the only investor in the deal. Reach out to your co-investors and get their input. Are they willing to fund deficits? Do they still have a strong feeling about the entrepreneur and the board? The next time you get a phone call about payroll, tell the entrepreneur that you'd like to get paid one day too!

210

For the Entrepreneur

No surprises. That's your main job as CEO once you are funded. Do everything you can to avoid asking investors to bail you out, especially with little notice. Contact late-paying customers and collect payment yourself; that will be an easier phone call to make. You want to keep your board members focused helping you in areas where they are stronger like management and market knowledge. Allow your backers to concentrate on factors that will improve the chances of a near-term exit for the company.

Make sure you are communicating constantly with investors and not just in the formal quarterly reports. If there are potential cash flow cliffs ahead, you want someone trained to spot them. Give them the information as soon as possible. If you want to call the angel on New Year's Eve, make sure it's to announce you've exceeded your revenue goals for the year or you're reached a milestone early. That's a call he wants to get.

Takeaway
Keep investors informed with the good, the bad and the ugly. The worst thing you can do is hide a problem and call an investor on a holiday to tell him you can't meet payroll this week.

97

Investment bankers are a great resource. Keep them informed

In the same way that you will network actively to generate and manage incoming deal flow for new investments, you can take a similar approach to generate interest among acquirers for a company to find an exit. Just as individual investors and angel groups have become more sophisticated and organized, investment bankers have become more specialized and interested in helping angels with deals.

With angel-only deals, building investment banker relationships ahead of time is important. You may start with a target list of several hundred investment bankers and narrow that down. Have a questionnaire to help you with the screening process. Ask about their preference for deal size; do any of the companies in your portfolio fit the criteria? Enlist other angels or angel groups in your network for referrals and assistance on refining your process.

Given that there is a lot of timing, expertise and chemistry associated with each deal, it is important to develop relationships with several investment bankers. As you get closer to an acquisition period, the skill set or industry experience you might require could change. It is not only the entrepreneur's responsibility, it is also your responsibility, to proactively push for an exit and to put together the right team to make it happen. Understand the specific milestones and inflection points the company will need to meet in order to gain strong interest for an acquisition in that industry. An investment banker can be extremely helpful in adding to those milestones. It can take anywhere from three to eighteen months to achieve an exit, and there's no guarantee things will go smoothly.

The right investment banker can help you create the selection criteria that identifies and screens potential acquirers, as well as manages the interview process. Take the time to align your goals with the different exit strategies, such as auctions. Make sure the entrepreneur and the management team understand the role of an investment banker versus a venture capitalist. Make sure they fully cooperate once the process begins. A good investment banker will allow the management team to stay focused on running the business.

Important: The board should actively negotiate terms with the investment banker. Many bankers require a retainer fee and a monthly minimum to actively solicit buyers. Sometimes you get what you pay for. If the company is tight on cash, investors may decide to fund the expense as a low-cost loan to the company. This is not a time to deplete cash out of the business; the company has to be firing on all cylinders to get a deal done.

For the Entrepreneur

You want your board monitoring your progress, not directly managing your company. To grow a start-up company to a successful exit with only one or two angel funding rounds means everyone has a significant role to play. Your focus is internally on the business, meeting product and market milestones. The board assists you with resources but is not responsible for the primary execution. Your board and any angel group or fund involved will mostly be focused externally, especially when they will be seeking potential acquirers and investment bankers to facilitate the exit. If you happen to know any investment bankers with merger and acquisition experience in your particular industry, introduce them to a board member. It's not always easy or fast to find the right fit with an investment banker. If an angel introduces an investment banker to you, make sure you treat him as you would one of your board members.

> **Definition of Investment Banker**
> A financial professional that can assists companies with merger and acquisition activity. Unlike venture capitalists, investment bankers engage at a transaction-based level and do not typically take an equity stake in the companies they represent. Some investment bankers require a monthly retainer to get engaged in a deal. Focus on investment bankers with success-based fees; you need as much capital as possible to stay in business.

98

Your founder flew to Fiji on Friday: step in when the CEO has a meltdown

What just happened? Did our founder really just take off for Fiji without warning? How could this happen now? Our investment banker has a deal on the table from a potential acquirer, and the key customers have strong ties to the founder. What did we miss? What do we do next? Did the entrepreneur really just experience a mental collapse that could derail the deal?

This scenario could happen to you as an angel. A complete meltdown with absolutely no notice, or possibly with warning bells you ignored. Maybe you eased up on monitoring because things appeared to be going so well or you had to put your attention on the potential acquisition. Now you can't get the deal done because it involves the CEO sticking around. If it falls apart now, you'll have to step in and run the company yourself. Aren't you glad you have years of management experience and planned for this as a contingency?

Exits can be very stressful times psychologically and physically for founders. Launching a company requires tremendous amounts of time and energy. Family relationships and friendships suffer. The founder's core identity as CEO is about to change; he'll either be working for the acquiring company with less authority, or he'll be out on his own trying to figure out what he's going to do next. He may be focused on everything that's gone wrong instead of the imminent success. The personal wealth he's about to realize through the acquisition may not come close to giving him the satisfaction of running his own business; it was never about the money. It was about the challenge, the ability to overcome high risk.

Exit stress and fatigue may trigger a personality shift you could have never predicted. Just as you design every investment for an exit, it's better to prepare for the off chance the founder may unexpectedly lose his way. Being prepared to step in the next day and navigate the company back on its intended course is part of being an investor.

For the Entrepreneur

What worries investors? It's the surprises, the unexpected blips and stalls that erode value subtly and keep you from reaching milestones. But mostly they are concerned about the mental condition of an entrepreneur right before an exit. Can you handle the stress? Would you ruin a deal at the eleventh hour? As we've explained elsewhere, this is when the investors are about to get paid for the risk they took to back you and your team.

You may not realize what the stress of growing the business has done to you, with having to make hundreds of business decisions every day, sacrificing family time and vacations to launch your company on a growth trajectory. Now, magnify that stress a hundredfold with a pending exit that puts even more pressure on your leadership abilities. Just know that your investors are prepared to step in right away and they do have the management experience and network of contacts to resolve whatever situation is presented. If you are having second thoughts, be up-front about it.

> **Takeaway**
> As the company moves toward an exit, it may be a good time to call on a coach to work with the board and the management team to go over responsibilities. It takes a team to get the company sold.

99

Always consider founder conflicts of interest and side deals

As an angel investor in a deal that is posed for an exit, you finally have time to reflect on the exceptional due diligence and board monitoring performed by the investor group. Have fun with those high-fives all around. But now is not the time to relax. You need to stay on top of the deal until the check clears the bank.

It's too easy in angel-only funded deal sizes for the entrepreneur, on his own, to lower the purchase price of the company in exchange for a higher salary and stock options in the acquiring company. Think about it like this: the entrepreneur went from owning 100% before you invested to now owning a much smaller percentage; a $200,000 raise or a guaranteed bonus may be better for the entrepreneur than an additional million dollars in the purchase price. In this scenario, the entrepreneur just took money out of your pocket and you probably didn't even realize it.

There are some ways to safeguard against this abuse. You could negotiate deal terms with a clause stipulating that a certain percentage of whatever the founder earns over the next five years, above a current salary, must be paid to the investors. That percentage is usually the pro rata share of ownership of the investors at the time of the sale. It could be difficult to block a founder if he owns a majority of the shares and can outvote you; however, since you most likely have to approve a sale, you do have some negotiating power.

This is why having a strong board is so critical. You're often so focused on getting the deal done and getting your money back, you aren't looking as diligently at any private conversations between the founder and the acquiring company. Remember, if you don't feel that the current board is strong enough to get the company through an exit with the investors' best interests in mind, replace them before it is too late. You need to be protected from these end-around moves.

For the Entrepreneur

If you agree to an angel investment, and are open to the benefits of board resources and monitoring, then don't make exceptions to that commitment. Everything needs to be out in the open, from the time of initial screening and due diligence before an investment is made, all the way through to striking a deal with an acquirer. If you are not putting in much cash up-front and using the investor's cash to get to an exit, you shouldn't be making side deals for yourself and your management team; that is detrimental to the sale price. Your fiduciary responsibility is to the board and your shareholders.

This is why you can expect sophisticated individual angels, angel groups and syndicates to have strong boards in place throughout the entire deal. Your integrity starts with the representations you made in the business plan and concludes when you help negotiate the sale of the business.

Takeaway
Watch out for side deals between entrepreneurs and an acquiring company. The board needs to stay on top of the negotiations to avoid any conflicts.

100

Bet on yourself

You may become frustrated. After several years as an angel, you either can't find enough interesting deals, enough co-investors to spread the risk, or your portfolio companies just aren't performing as well as you'd like. You may wonder: is it possible to even make money at this?

Here's a suggestion. Go start a company. Do it yourself and see if it can still be done. Invest in your own ability to get to an exit and prove success.

Identify people who have had a level of success working together, and assemble a small team. Make sure you're all accountable to each other, and then give yourself the freedom to fail. Set a short time horizon to exit and agree that an exit equals success.

Put in some of your own money, but don't take outside money. If the company needs more capital, provide your own infusions. Bet on yourself. You may be surprised at your success! Get in and get out!

Tools: Glossary of Terms

A

Accredited Investor –As of 2013, the U.S. Securities & Exchange Commission defined an accredited investor in Rule 501 of Regulation D as:
- $1 million or more in net worth, or joint net worth with the person's spouse, excluding the primary residence; or,
- Personal income in excess of $200,000 in each of the last two years; or,
- Joint income with a spouse exceeding $300,000 over the same time period and a reasonable expectation of the same income level in the current year.

Angel Groups – Funds or networks formed for the purpose of pooling the knowledge and capital of accredited investors to make private investments in start-up and early-stage companies.

Angel Investors – Accredited investors with an interest in providing human and financial capital to entrepreneurial companies with many different goals.

Anti-Dilution Provisions – Depending on the definition set in the term sheet, this mechanism preserves an investor's ownership percentage in a subsequent round of funding and provides protection in the event of a stock split or other recapitalization.

Automatic Conversion – If a company goes public or a majority of the investors in a certain round of investment vote to convert, an investor's shares will be converted 1:1 into common shares.

B

Bridge Financing – Typically used by companies seeking a small amount of capital to support operations while raising the next round of funding. In most cases, investors and companies will use convertible notes in the form of debt that is converted into equity once the next round closes.

Brokers – Licensed firms or individuals who charge a fee to early-stage companies to help raise funds from private investors and funds. Many angel investors will not look at deals if a broker is involved.

C

C-Corporation – The preferred legal structure of a company seeking funds. C-corporations protect shareholders from liability in the event of a legal issue or bankruptcy. Most companies prefer to be registered in Delaware; although, it is possible to register a C-Corporation in your state.

Call – A call option gives a company the right to force an investor to sell his shares.

Cap Table – The capitalization of the company provides the legal names and shares owned by founders, investors, and other stakeholders. The table provides an overview of each investment round and defines outstanding options, warrants, and unallocated shares.

Capital Reserves – Angels have a finite amount of money to allocate to early-stage investments (typically 5% of net worth.) Angels need their portfolio companies to exit, profitably, in order to keep playing in this space. Angels should resist putting all of their early-stage investable dollars in only one deal; the risk of failure increases significantly. (See Dry Powder)

Clawback – If the valuation negotiation is difficult, many investors will offer an entrepreneur the ability to recapture ownership in the company if certain milestones and objectives are met. If used, this provision must be clearly defined in the term sheet and closing documents.

Common Stock – Most companies will have both common and preferred stock. Common stock is traditionally held by founders and used almost exclusively for board and employee options. Common shares are subordinate to preferred shares.

Conversion Rights – This is a provision outlining the rights or obligation of investors to convert preferred shares to common stock. Conversion may be executable at the time of an IPO, if certain sales targets are hit, or a supermajority of preferred stockholders vote to convert to common.

Convertible Debt – A debt instrument (such as a promissory note) that can be converted to equity of the issuer (either as common stock or preferred stock) at a predetermined discount, with or without nominal interest, in a future round of funding.

Convertible Note – Convertible notes are often used when the valuation of the company cannot be negotiated or determined. A convertible note is structured in such a way that interest is usually accumulated and, upon the next round of financing, will convert to common or preferred shares at a discount. The discount, interest rate, and maturity date are negotiated in the terms.

Convertible Preferred Stock – Holders of this class of stock, usually Angels and Venture Capital Funds, have preference over the common shareholders in the event of a liquidation event. (See Participating Preferred)

Cram Down – A financing round at a valuation less than a previous round of investment. The ownership of previous investors will be diluted.

D

D&O Insurance – The actual name is Directors' and Officers' Insurance. Most investors require portfolio companies to carry this policy as a means to protect board members from lawsuits and to cover the costs of legal expenses associated with claims.

Deal Structure – Typically defined in the term sheet, the structure of a deal is memorialized in a Purchase Agreement between investors and the company to define the rights and obligations of all parties.

Demand Registration Rights – A provision in the deal that allows investors to convert ownership in the company, through registration, to shares eligible for trading on the public market.

Dilution – A reduction in investors' ownership in a company as a result of a subsequent round of financing. Investors may retain their ownership in a company by making additional investments in subsequent rounds of financing.

Discounted Cash Flow – Highly-theoretical valuation method projecting a company's ability to generate cash at a future point, then discounting it to determine the present value.

Dividends – While not mandatory, some investors will require that dividends are paid on the money they invest. Dividends can be paid either in cash, at a future date, or as additional shares. Dividends may or may not be cumulative.

Down Round – If the price per share is less than in the previous round of investment, an investor will experience dilution and a cram down. (See Cram Down)

Dry Powder – Reserved and/or committed capital that creates a financial cushion in case the deal needs more funding than expected. Dry powder is formally allocated by angel investors in recognition of the longer time periods and unanticipated expenses required to make an early-stage company attractive to an acquirer and exit successfully. In most cases, the investor has the right not to make a follow-on investment.

Due Diligence – Experienced investors create a pre-defined checklist and process to determine if a deal can work. Some items may include reviewing the business plan, the financials, the market, the competition, the technology, the management team, the operating plan, the intellectual property, the exit strategy, and so forth. Many angels will join a syndicate to spread out the work and to get access to industry-experts from other investor groups.

E

Equity – Ownership interest in a company in the form of stock or stock options.

Elevator Pitch – A ninety-second summary used to quickly and simply define a product or service and its value proposition, literally in the amount of time it would take to deliver on an elevator ride.

Exit Strategy – Most investors in early-stage companies get paid upon an exit. The exit strategy is an important part of determining the valuation of the company before making the first investment. The board, investors, and entrepreneur must be on the same page to be successful. Most exits do not involve taking the company public (IPO).

F

First Close – Depending on the size of a round and the ability of the company to execute, some investors may be willing to write a check early, before all the money in the round is verified and committed. Most investors, who are willing to close early, believe strongly in the deal or have set a minimum funding requirement that has been met.

First Refusal Rights –A term defined in the closing documents that provides the company or existing shareholders with the obligation to sell shares to the company or existing shareholders at a previously negotiated price or the fair market value prior to seeking outside buyers for their shares.

Forced Buyback – See Redemption Right.

Founder Vesting – Key personnel may be required to vest their original shares, over a defined period of time, in a company when the first institutional round of investment is received. Typically the time period is three to four years and is fully-vested upon a liquidation event. The goal of vesting founders' shares is to keep key personnel engaged with the company.

Fully Diluted – Total number of common shares and preferred shares outstanding, including: stock options, warrants, and convertible notes.

H

Hockey Stick – An unfounded and untested growth assumption represented on a revenue chart as a long flat line that veers upward suddenly at the very end. Financial projections, developed by entrepreneurs, often show a large and unrealistic spike in revenue in year 5 to justify higher valuations.

I

Information Rights – Many investors require this provision to force companies to provide financial and board updates on a quarterly or yearly basis. If this provision is not in the final closing documents, the entrepreneur may not be required to provide data to minority shareholders in a private company.

Initial Public Offering (IPO) – A non-traditional exit strategy for angel funded deals. An IPO refers to taking a private company public. Most companies are required to file an S-1 to announce its intentions. In some special situations, companies have been known to do a reverse IPO where it purchases a public shell company.

Intellectual Property (IP) – Includes patents, trademarks, copyrights, and other license agreements that may represent a strategic advantage for a company. This should be a major due diligence item for investors to review before making an investment decision.

Internal Rate of Return (IRR) – The rate of return on an investment based on the amount of time and total value of the exit. A 15% IRR over 5 years means that the investor received a 2x multiple on their investment. The higher the IRR, the better the return.

Investment Bankers – A financial professional that can assists companies with merger and acquisition activity. Unlike venture capitalists, investment bankers engage at a transaction-based level and do not typically take an equity stake in the companies they represent. Some investment bankers require a monthly retainer to get engaged in a deal. Focus on investment bankers with success-based fees to conserve cash.

L

Lead Investor – A lead investor may be the most experienced, the one with the largest funds, or an expert in the specific industry of the early-stage deal that the syndicate is reviewing in due diligence.

Lifestyle Business – A small commercial enterprise operated more for the owner's enjoyment and satisfaction than for the profit it earns or its high-growth, wealth-creation potential. Investors are not so sure about the "quality of life" argument espoused by lifestyle business owners. Investors believe that angel funded deals create an even higher quality of living for the entrepreneur's family.

Limited Liability Company (LLC) – Similar to a C-Corporation in that there is limited liability for members (owners); however, a LLC also has additional tax advantages. Some investors and funds will not invest in early-stage deals that are formed as a LLC.

Liquidation Preference – Amount repaid to an investor when the company is liquidated (sold), defined as a multiple of capital invested.

M

Majority – Defines the percentage of the majority of shareholders that must approve actions before the company can proceed with such things as selling, merging with, or acquiring a business. Majority is typically defined as 50% or more.

Mezzanine Financing – For growth companies with consistent revenue, this type of funding may be available to provide expansion funds. Mezzanine funding typically requires an above market interest rate and is typically short-term.

N

Non-Disclosure Agreement (NDA) – An agreement which does not allow the disclosure of certain information to third-parties over a defined period of time. Most investors will not sign a NDA.

O

Over-Subscribed – In the event that a round of funding is over-subscribed, current investors may be limited to their prorata share of the new financing round. The board or entrepreneur may vote to expand the round and to accept additional funds that could be useful to expand the business.

P

Participating Preferred – The right of an investor to first receive capital back when a company is sold, then participate in the sale based upon pro rata share of the common stock.

Pay-to-Play – A requirement in some venture capital and angel investments. If a preferred shareholder desires to maintain certain rights as a preferred stockholder, he must participate and invest pro rata in future financings or lose those rights.

Penny Warrants – Securities that give stockholders the right, but not the obligation to buy shares of common stock at a fixed price over a specified period of time. Penny warrants have a strike price of $0.01 per share. (See Warrants)

Post-Money Valuation – The valuation of the company, on a fully-diluted basis, immediately after all funding is received. The valuation is the pre-money valuation plus any funds received.

Pre-Money Valuation – The valuation of the company immediately before an investment.

Preferred Stock – Most investors require preferred stock since it is senior to common stock. However, most preferred stock is subordinate to any outstanding bank or debt financing. Preferred stock may have liquidation rights, voting rights, and additional provisions that are not shared by holders of common stock.

Private Placement Memorandum (PPM) – A formal document that complies with federal securities regulations. A PPM is not recommended to entrepreneurs since most accredited investors may require their own deal structure. A PPM is not required to sell shares to accredited investors.

Protective Provisions – Allows certain shareholders to veto certain actions, such as selling the company or raising additional rounds of capital or changing the number of board members. They can protect the preferred minority shareholders (typically the angel investors) from unfair actions by the common majority (founders).

Put – A put option gives the investor the right to force the company to purchase his shares.

R

Redemption Rights – Allows the investor the ability to force the company to liquidate the original investment at a pre-determined price if the company does not reach a liquidation event (exit) in a specified period of time.

Registration – The process for the company to be authorized by the Securities and Exchange Commission (SEC) to sell shares to the public.

Registration Rights – A provision in the purchase agreement that allow investors to sell stock via the public market after a set period of time typically defined by a lock-up period.

Return on Investment (ROI) - The multiple or return on an investment. As an example, if an angel invested $10,000 in a deal and received $50,000 when the company was sold, that angel received a 5x multiple on their investment. The ROI does not calculate timing.

Rounds of Funding – Companies seeking capital from investors will raise funds in a series of rounds. Initial funding will be a seed round that is followed by Series A, Series B, and so forth as needed. Typically, entrepreneurs will have the most difficulty raising early funds because of the limited operational history of the business.

Rule 504 – The Security and Exchange Commission (SEC) provides an exemption, in Regulation D, from the registration requirements of the federal securities laws for some companies when they offer and sell up to $1,000,000 of their securities in any 12-month period.

Rule 505 – The Security and Exchange Commission (SEC) allows some companies offering their securities to have those securities exempted from the registration requirements of the federal securities laws. To qualify for this exemption, a company can only sell up to $5 million in a 12-month period to an unlimited number of accredited investors and up to 35 investors, without soliciting, who do not meet the accredited standards.

S

S-Corporation – An S-Corporation is not a recommended form of incorporation for an entrepreneur who may need to raise funds from angels, angel groups, or venture capital funds.

Screening – Many individual investors and angel funds use a screening process to determine their interest in deals. Screening may be formal or informal. Screening may involve presenting to a fund manager or to an entire group. Most entrepreneurs should find out the specific screening process and be sure to comply with the rules.

Seed or Start-up Financing – Small amount of capital to allow an entrepreneur to prove and to execute on a concept. Additional rounds of financing are typically referred to using an alphabetical system: Series A, Series B, Series C and so on. Angel investors typically invest in seed, Series A, or Series B rounds. See Dry Powder for more information.

Stock Options – Founders, employees, board members, and advisors may be granted options to purchase common stock at a specific exercise price over a certain period of time. These options are often used as additional incentive to keep salaries low and to preserve cash.

Subordinated Debt – Investors need to remember that debt instruments used to fund the company will be subordinated to bank debt. If the company begins to fail, the bank will receive its money first, then debt holders, then preferred stockholders, and then common stockholders.

Supermajority – Defines the percentage of the majority of shareholders that must approve actions before the company can proceed with such things as selling, merging with, or acquiring a business. Supermajority is typically defined as 66.67% or more.

Syndication – The process of bringing together several investors or lenders to fund a company. Investors in a syndicate may be legally-bound to make future capital investments if defined in the closing documents. A syndicate is not limited to equity investors; it can be a combination of debt and equity players.

T

Term Sheet – A document that outlines the key terms of a proposed transaction. It also provides information that will be used as the basis for the deal documents, including the capitalization table, legal terms and the rights of all parties. The term sheet is typically non-binding, except for certain provisions.

Tranche – Many investors will hold back on their investments and only fund a partial amount of a round to limit the risk involved with certain milestones that the company is pursuing. If the company is successful with those milestones, the closing documents may have triggers that automatically call the next investment from investors. Tranching lowers risk.

V

Venture (Vulture) Capitalist – Unlike angel investors, Venture Capitalists typically invest institutional money (other people's money) in deals. While Venture Capitalists may have certain skillsets and industry knowledge, they typically will use paid consultants to assist on due diligence. VCs invest much larger amounts of money in each deal than angels.

Vesting Schedule – The timing and mechanism required to release shares to founders, employees, board members, and other stakeholders. Traditionally, all shares become fully-vested in the event of an early-exit. (See Founder Vesting)

Voting Rights – The rights of a shareholder to vote. Votes may be held on electing a board or on the sale of a company or certain assets. Investors may vote directly or as a class. Investors should be cognizant of their rights and the voting percentage required for specific acts to be approved. The term sheet and closing documents, at the most recent funding round, will outline how a majority or supermajority is defined.

W

Warrants – Securities that give stockholders the right, but not the obligation to buy shares of common stock at a fixed price over a specified period of time. Warrants are similar to stock options and offered to investors (or to service providers in exchange for fees.)

1202 Stock – Provides a special tax treatment on capital gains by reducing the long-term capital gains tax by 50% on portfolio companies held for five years or more.

1244 Stock – Provides tax relief to investors by allowing them to deduct up to $50,000, or $100,000 if filed with a spouse, against ordinary income in a year if they suffered a loss from the sale or liquidation of a small business.

About the Authors

Michael Cain is the founder, investor, and managing partner of Wilmington Investor Network, LLC, an angel investment fund he formed in July 2004. He is a founder and managing Partner of Guardant Partners, LLC, an investment management partnership and also a managing partner of their special situations fund located in Greensboro, North Carolina. He is an investor and former manager of Emergent Growth Fund Two in Gainesville, Florida. His angel funds have invested in excess of $25 million in over 40 early stage startup companies. Each investment requires continuing angel involvement, mentorship, advice, and consultation.

Cain is Chairman of the Angel Resource Institute (ARI), a non-profit angel research and education foundation originally created and funded by the Kauffman Foundation of Kansas City. ARI is the sister organization to the Angel Capital Association, comprised of over 180 U.S. based angel groups representing thousands of active early-stage angel investors. Cain remains Vice Chairman of The Atlantis group, a fully invested angel fund based in Durham, NC. He also serves on several for-profit and non-profit boards. Prior to becoming a full-time angel investor in 1995, Cain started, operated, and successfully exited a variety of businesses. The companies included computer software sales and service, drying equipment, and the paper industry. During the 1980's, he developed a 28 store regional Wendy's Franchise.

Cain received his Juris Doctor degree from Syracuse University School of Law and his Bachelor of Arts in Political Science from the University of Vermont. Prior to becoming a full-time entrepreneur, he practiced commercial law and was a States Attorney Prosecutor in Vermont.

D. Troy Knauss is a partner in a number of Angel funds and networks that invest in early-stage, high-growth and turnaround companies. Knauss has over 20 years of experience in family, growth, and start-up businesses. In addition to his fund activities, Knauss is a multi-exited entrepreneur with start-up and growth management experience in food processing, marketing and brand building, software development, and eCommerce sales channels. Knauss is an active early-stage angel investor in multiple companies and serves as Executive Chairman on a number of Boards.

Knauss was named one of the Triad's Impact Entrepreneurs by Business Leader magazine. He speaks frequently to investors and entrepreneurs on private investing around the globe, serves on the Board of Trustees, and, as President for the Angel Resource Institute, is a former Board member of the Angel Capital Association and an adjunct professor at Wake Forest University, is active on for-profit Boards, and volunteers on a number of non-profit entrepreneurial boards and committees that help promote the start-up community.

Knauss holds an undergraduate degree in Business Administration from Susquehanna University and a Masters of Business Administration from Wake Forest University.

Notes

Notes

63843409R00131

Made in the USA
Lexington, KY
19 May 2017